STO

ACPL
DISCARDED

P9-ELH-637

6-9-60

NOV 3 0 '60

3-16-61

The Minister
in Christian Education

The Minister
in Christian Education

by
Peter P. Person

BAKER BOOK HOUSE
Grand Rapids 6, Michigan
1960

Copyright, 1960, by
BAKER BOOK HOUSE

Library of Congress Catalog Card Number: 60-10190

Printed in the United States of America

1121560

Preface

The title of this book, *The Minister in Christian Education*, suggests the author's point of view. The pastor is not a critical observer looking in upon Christian education; he is on the inside acting as an interested participant. As administrative head of the local church he is responsible for the educational ministry sponsored by his church.

We offer no apologies for the fact that the book is of a popular rather than a scholarly nature. We deliberately planned it so. Its aim is to be practical rather than profound, and is written with the average pastor serving an average church in mind. Readers who crave a scientific approach will find at the end of each chapter a list of a few such books. These *suggested readings* include titles both old and new, in fact some of the listed books are out of print. They are, however, available in second-hand book stores and pastors are known to be good customers of such shops. The fact that a book is out of print does not mean that it is out of date. Some of these old books are classics in Christian education.

No attempt has been made to screen titles and label them as to their theological and philosophical points of view. We have listed authors with whom we disagree, but pastors should be mentally and emotionally mature enough to judge for themselves. "By all means use your judgment and hold on to whatever is really good. Steer clear of evil in any form" (I Thessalonians 5:21, 22, Phillips).

P.P.P.

April 1960

Contents

Introduction

The seminary senior dreams about his future church while the retired pastor dreams about his past pastorates. The one is anticipation, the other is reminiscence; both are colored with idealism. Dreaming is an inexpensive innocent pastime, but if dreams become a retreat from reality in an effort to escape present responsibilities, they cease to be innocent.

The retired pastor basks in the happy memories of a golden past, the good old days. His ministerial mistakes are glossed over, if not altogether forgotten, while his achievements tend to become magnified. His mental image of his ministry becomes more like an oil painting than a candid camera shot. But dreams are subjective and very personal and should not be seen through the eyes of objective science. Let the retired pastor enjoy dreaming about his pastoral past as long as he does not insist that the young pastor must adopt the same patterns.

The seminarian's dreams focus on the pulpit. That is quite natural for three reasons. *First* of all, the mass media of pulpit oratory is far more dramatic than house to house visitation, or teaching a Bible class in Sunday school. In the *second* place, he has probably been captivated by the personality of some eloquent preacher and both consciously and unconsciously has come to imitate his manners and peculiarities. The *third* reason is that his seminary education has been largely pulpit centered. He has been trained to preach. It is quite natural, therefore, for him to dream of himself occupying the pulpit of a large urban church with an assistant to do the pastoral calling, a director of parish education to care for the ministry to the children and youth and an efficient office secretary. He is thus free to devote himself to his study in preparation for his pulpit appearances. His dream includes a modern manse with a charming mistress of the Manse. "All this and heaven too!"

But he is apt to have a rude, not to say cruel, awakening from his dream after graduation, when he finds himself not in the church of his dreams but in one of God's many back pastures. He soon discovers that people are not crowding to hear him speak for God; he is a shepherd whose primary task seems to be to seek straying sheep and lost lambs. In the pulpit he feels more perspiration than inspiration. Discouraged and dejected, he asks himself — "Is this what the ministry is like? Why wasn't I warned what I might expect?"

During my early teaching ministry, a young friend who had been away from the seminary campus long enough to sample some of the realism of the ministry made a comment in the course of our conversation that disturbed me. "Why don't the teachers in the seminary tell their students what to expect? It would spare them from being painfully disillusioned when they become pastors." That remark continued to disturb me. Perhaps our presentation of the ministerial calling is too idealistic; maybe we should be more realistic. As I mulled over the matter, I came to feel that it was my duty to present the prosaic facts. On an otherwise dark and dreary day I devoted an entire class period to presenting an almost morbid picture of the ministry. My students listened attentively until the class bell announced the close of the session. As they left the classroom, one student paused at my desk. I can still see him. There was a look of grim determination on his face and a ring of sincerity in his voice as he volunteered his vow. "If what you have said this morning is true, and I suppose it is, we can expect some rugged experiences. But," he added with conviction "I am determined to go through with it." Brave words for a first year seminary student. I have never forgotten that session though nearly a quarter of a century has elapsed. He is still an active pastor. He has never served a large church but wherever he has served, he has been faithful. To him the words of Jesus would well apply, "Well done thou good and faithful servant."

Winston Churchill in the early days of the second world war warned his people that they must be prepared for *blood, sweat,* and *tears.* Jesus warned his disciples that they would experience *persecutions, trials,* and *tribulation.* In both instances, these sobering words became an accepted challenge. The gospel ministry is no bed of roses. The words of Paul to his young friend and co-minister, Timothy, may well apply to our young pastors of today, "Endure hardship as a good soldier of Christ Jesus" (II Timothy 2:3).

The seminary student preparing for services in the foreign mission field usually receives a realistic training for his task. The teachers are usually former missionaries who can share firsthand experiences from the mission field with these prospective missionaries. The missionary candidates are carefully screened. The idea that those who can not qualify for the ministry in the home field are sent as missionaries to the foreign field is a bit of vicious fiction. Missionary training schools and the departments of missions in the theological seminaries have tended to be more practical than theoretical. That, however, does not mean that they have resorted to coaching rather than to educating.

At the turn of the century a new type of professional training for the ministry emerged, *religious education.* Church sponsored colleges and universities established departments of religious education granting bachelors', masters', and even doctors' degrees. A few seminaries added departments of religious education but most of them continued their traditional curricula with the addition of a few courses, mostly electives. There were two main reasons for the development of this new type of education. *First,* the phenomenal growth of the Sunday School movement. In America, it was a generally accepted institution. Liberal as well as conservative churches, small as well as large churches conducted Sunday Schools. The lack of standards and direction was evident. There were glaring violations of pedagogical principles and a lack of understanding of child and adolescent psychology. There was a crying need for professional leadership in this lay movement of the church. The *second* reason was basically one of theology. During the nineteenth century, the New England revivalism was first questioned and then challenged. Horace Bushnell's book, *Christian Nurture,* was freely quoted and often misquoted. The theological debate centered around Nature versus Nurture; was conversion necessary or would Christian culture suffice? Many church leaders, among them pastors, advocated religious education as a desirable substitute for revivalism. The very term *religious education* thus became anathema to the more conservative groups. A new term had been coined, *directors of religious education*. Young women as well as young men took this professional training. As the conservative churches came to realize the value of trained leadership in the teaching ministry, they too established training courses. They could adopt new methods of teaching without changing the contents of the curricula. Pastors in both liberal and conservative churches welcomed the assistance of professionally trained workers with children and youth. The parents, too, came to appreciate what was done for their children. Then came the unforeseen economic depression of the thirties. The new movement suffered a crippling blow. Church budgets had to be drastically cut, paid personnel had to be reduced. The educational work had to be taken over either by the pastor himself or volunteer untrained workers. The trained directors were dropped, not because their work was not appreciated, but because there were no funds for their salaries. As a matter of necessity, these professional religious educators had to seek their living in other vocations.

Within recent years the interest in the movement has revived. We now have directors of parish education, of Christian education, of children's work, and of youth work. Our larger churches are staffed by salaried professionally trained directors. We are living in an age of specialization even in the work of the church. Most theological seminaries have added social work and counseling to their curricula, but very few of them have as yet taken seriously the responsibility of training for Christian education.

The small church cannot afford to engage a staff of professional workers to assist the pastor. In these circumstances the pastor must either surrender the educational ministry to a Sunday School superintendent and his staff of untrained teachers or he must assume the responsibility of being director as well as pastor. Unfortunately he was not trained for this task in his seminary course. The result is that he flounders around rather than gives leadership. His lack of information can be remedied, at least in part, through the reading of current books and magazines dealing with Christian education, but he still feels his lack of professional training.

When a new pastor comes to an old church, he may find that its program of education is limited to Sunday sessions so lacking in educational standards that they do not deserve the name *school*. The congregation is satisfied with the status quo. The church lives largely in the past, it is a Sunday to Sunday existence without any plans for the future. There seems to be no aggressive leadership within its membership.

The disillusioned new pastor, keenly interested in the teaching ministry of the church, may resign himself to what he considers a hopeless situation. He marks time from Sunday to Sunday hoping and praying for a call from a more promising church. Or he may decide upon a radical reformation. He reorganizes the Sunday School, even rewrites the constitution of the church. The congregation is carried into a building project for which it is neither financially nor emotionally ready. He puts new life into the old church. When after a brief pastorate he moves to a new field of activity he leaves a new building, but the congregation is left with a crippling debt. He has reorganized the church but the machinery is so complicated that no one can run it now after he, the engineer, has gone.

There is still another approach to the problem. The new pastor may take an inventory of the available resources of the old church. He need not forsake his idealism as he faces reality. There is not much to work with, but there is something. Rome was not built in a day nor is a modern program of Christian education introduced into a local church at one session of the congregation nor at two. He must first of all win the confidence of his members. He must encourage them in what they are attempting to do. Subtly he plants ideas in the minds of the more progressive members. He carefully avoids moving faster than his congregation is able to follow. Progress is painfully slow but gradually improvement is evident. He has helped them to see their potentialities as well as their limitations. His attitude has not been that of a boss cracking the whip over their heads, nor a director giving orders. He has been a participant sharing with his workers the planning as well as the implementing of a program adequate for their needs. In the book of Ezra (5:2) there is an interesting reference to the participation of the prophets Haggai and Zechariah in the rebuilding of the Jerusalem temple. Zerubbabel and Jeshua were the leaders in the project but "with them were the prophets of God, helping them." The church of today is in need of such practical prophets.

Whether the church is large or small, urban or rural, the pastor is the key person in the program of Christian education. His attitude will either inspire or discourage the workers. Enthusiasm is contagious, but so is also indifference. Even the pastor who has professional directors on his staff cannot afford to retreat from his responsibility in the educational program. He may not directly participate in the teaching program, but he should be informed as to its nature and progress. This book is written primarily for the pastor who is his own director of Christian education but who recruits and trains fellow workers from the membership of his own church; but we are also concerned that all pastors should have an active interest in Christian education, even though they have professional educators on their staff.

1
The Teaching Ministry
of the Church

The Christian church is commissioned to teach, but its pastors are not always committed to the teaching ministry. Jesus in his missionary mandate commanded his disciples to go forth making disciples of all nations baptizing and *teaching* them (cf. Matthew 28:16-20). Paul, the aged apostle, in writing to his young friend Timothy admonished him to entrust the gospel to faithful men who were "apt to teach" (II Timothy 2:24). He is to teach the "holy Scriptures" (II Timothy 3:14-17). The Apostolic church was a teaching church (Acts 5:42).

But teaching is not the only mission of the church. In his message to the household of the Roman military officer, Cornelius, Peter refers to Jesus as one who "went about doing good and healing all that were oppressed of the devil" (Acts 10:38). Matthew 9:35 records a summary of Jesus' ministry; *teaching, preaching,* and *healing.* Paul refers to himself as being divinely appointed to a three-fold ministry, as *preacher, apostle,* and *teacher* (II Timothy 1:11). If the twentieth century church is to fulfill its task, it must be concerned with preaching, teaching, and a social ministry. Any attempt to compare these ministries in terms of importance would be folly, for all three are important. Since the pastor is the head of the local church, he should be concerned with all three areas. While recognizing the importance of both the pulpit and the social work of the pastor, we shall devote our thinking primarily to the pastor's place in the educational program of the church.

Whom shall we teach?

The words of Jesus are explicit, *"all nations."* We have in-

terpreted the words *all nations* to mean foreign nations, people
who live far away beyond the oceans, Africa, China, Japan, and
the millions of India — forgetting that the *all* includes our own
nation as well. Jesus sketched the proposed progress of this
teaching ministry in his final words to his disciples (Acts 1:8),
Jerusalem, Judea, Samaria, and the end of the earth ("uttermost part of the earth," ASV). They were to begin at home
and then expand their ministry to the uttermost part of the
earth. If we neglect the Jerusalem area, the end of the earth
will eventually suffer. Our field embraces the whole wide world.
A saintly old woman used to conclude her very lengthy prayers
with a rather strange petition "God bless all the peoples in the
whole world — and in Chicago, too." We thought of her as
being a simple minded saint, but perhaps she was more alert
than we realized. She had learned that as Chicagoans, it was so
easy to forget Chicago when we prayed for all nations; she
wanted to make certain that God remembered her city.

Our teaching is to extend to all ages as well as to all nations.
We are so accustomed to associating the term *children* with
teaching, that we often forget that the teaching program of the
church should include all ages "from the cradle to the grave."
The Sunday School came into being to minister to underprivileged children in England and is still considered, even by
some pastors in America, to be a Sunday religious school for
children. The modern Sunday School provides for all ages from
the nursery to the older adults. Church sponsored adult education is not limited to classes held on Sunday.

The family in Christian education

The immediate responsibility of the church is to the families
that constitute the local congregation. To the Philippian jailer's
question, "What must I do to be saved?" Paul replied, "Believe
on the Lord Jesus Christ and thou shalt be saved, and thy house"
(Acts 16:31). Note also Acts 10:2; 11:14; 18:8; I Corinthians
1:16; John 4:53. Becoming a disciple of Christ is a personal
rather than group response, yet one cannot thoughtfully study
the book of Acts without sensing the stress that is placed upon

the *family* commitment to Christ. In our evangelical Protestant churches we have individualized the Christian life, often neglecting the social implications of the family. With our modern emphasis on grading and grouping for worship as well as for instruction, we are in real danger of losing the traditional family pew. There are many modern religious educators who consider the family pew as a mere old tradition without survival value, but there are others who place a high value on the social significance of the worship of the family as a unit. In America today there are countless numbers of families where the parents are devout Christians and loyal church members, yet their children have become prodigal sons and daughters. This is even true in some pastor's families. Perhaps the parents have taken too much for granted. Like Mary and Joseph, they have "supposed" that their child was "in the company" (Luke 2:44). We help to evangelize the children of the natives in distant Africa, but we neglect to evangelize those that live under the same roof, and eat at the same table. With the prophet Isaiah, may Christian parents be able to report to the Father of all mankind "Behold I and the children which God hath given me" (Hebrews 2:13; Isaiah 8:17, 18).

Then there are *fringe families*. The children attend Sunday School regularly; the parents are not members of the church, but they attend services occasionally; they even contribute to the support of the church. They evidence an outsider's interest in the church. They are interested in having their children receive Christian instruction, but they themselves have not made a personal commitment to Christ. Some are seekers after truth, but they have not yet discovered Christ as their personal Lord and Saviour. Experience has taught us that unless we win the family for Christ and the church, we will very often lose the children when they come to the age of adolescence. We must strive to win the families as well as the children.

Within the parish and often in the very shadow of the church, there are pagan families. In some of these homes, there is profanity, gambling, and drunkenness; in others there may be culture and refinement, but a total absence of Christian prin-

ciples. The one type of family needs the gospel just as much as
the other. They are located within the parish and are the responsibility of the local church. It is a pagan mission field at
our very doors. When we pray for the heathen in distant lands,
let us not forget our pagan neighbors. If they will not come to
the church, then the church must go to them with the gospel.
Recruiting the children for the Sunday School may serve as an
opening wedge in such homes. It is often easier to reach the
pagans in distant lands with the gospel than to evangelize those
in our own parishes.

With the phenomenal growth of our modern cities, new sub-
divisions are mushrooming. Young couples with small children
locate in these suburbs, buying or building their own homes.
They may thus be locating many miles from the home church.
For a time they continue to attend the home church, bringing
their children to Sunday School. Before long, their pastor discovers that they are more often absent than present at the
regular church services, and the children are often absent from
Sunday School. He visits their home and discovers that they live
beyond the limits of his parish. What shall the pastor do? Shall
he reprimand them for their church delinquency, tactfully try
to motivate them to become more faithful in church attendance,
or shall he subtly suggest that for the sake of their spiritual welfare, the family affiliate with some church in their new neighborhood? Is the pastor more concerned with losing a family
from his church roll than he is in the family's spiritual welfare?
"Displaced" young families often become church delinquents,
gradually losing their spiritual interests. "The cares of this
world, and the deceitfulness of riches, and the lust of other
things" choke their spiritual lives (Mark 4:19). Bringing children to Sunday School from outgoing areas may contribute to
keep up the Sunday School enrollment, but it has been discovered that children "bussed" to Sunday School usually drop
out during High School years.

The teaching ministry of the local church must reach beyond
Jerusalem, Judea, and Samaria to the ends of the earth. But
how? Future missionaries are now being taught in our local

Sunday School classes, they are learning leadership through participation in the youth organizations of the church. Those who are to become the financial supporters of the missionary program of the church are being, or should be, educated in stewardship and participation in world missions, through the local church.

Adults, too, need to be informed about the purpose and program of world missions. Often the missionary education in the local church is limited to occasional visits by returned missionaries who by means of oral description, native costumes, and pictures dramatize the work they represent. An hour of such missionary stimulus may result in a good collection for missions, but contributes very little to an understanding of the total plan, purpose, and problems of world missions. It is an emotional rather than an educational approach.

Who shall teach?

Granting that the local church is commissioned to teach, we face the question, *Who shall teach?* The pastor is called both to preach and to teach. He is therefore directly responsible for the teaching ministry of the church. In a subsequent chapter, we shall discuss the pastor as an educator. But who besides the pastor is responsible for the teaching? Moses in Deuteronomy 6 gives a definite command to the fathers to teach their own children. It was religious education in the family; it was to be continuous and not a mere five minutes of daily family devotions. In our modern American homes the responsibility seems to have been largely shifted from the fathers to the mothers who in their turn shift the responsibility to the Sunday School teachers. No church class room, no matter how ideal, can take the place of the Christian home, and no Sunday School teacher, no matter how devoted, can be an adequate substitute for a truly Christian mother. Christian parents must assume their God-given place in the teaching ministry.

In most churches, it is the Sunday School teacher who is considered the official teacher in the educational program of the local church. These teachers are volunteers, receiving no monetary remuneration for their services. Most of them have had no professional training for their teaching task. It has been a case of learning by doing. The leadership courses taken by some of these teachers could perhaps more correctly be called coaching than educational sessions. It is being told *what* to do rather than to be given reasons *why*.

Then, too, there are counselors and lay directors of youth activities. In larger churches, there are salaried professionally trained directors of Christian education. Their titles vary in the different churches; directors of Christian education, directors of children's work, youth pastors, etc. The pastor besides being responsible for the teaching ministry of his staff is himself a teacher. In the pulpit his messages are often of a didactic nature; he may be teaching a class in the Sunday School; he may be teaching in the midweek service. He is the key person in the teaching program of the church even though he may be assisted by trained educational leaders.

What shall we teach?

The Bible

The traditional answer, *the Bible,* is a more pious than practical answer, for the Bible is a religious source book rather than an organized textbook. Then, too, there is much extra-Biblical information that needs to be presented and assimilated. Since the Bible is our basic directive for Christian thought and life, familiarity with its content and interpretation is imperative in any program of evangelical Christian education.

For the small child, we select Bible stories and paraphrase them into the child's vocabulary. These stories are presented both orally and pictorially. Bible story books are sold in practically all general book stores; even drug stores and "five and ten cent" stores display them.

The primary child who is just learning to read should be given a small New Testament with pictures. Many of the words are beyond the vocabulary range of the child, but it means much to him to actually own a "Bible." The Junior should have a whole Bible all his own. Printing his name in gold on the cover costs only a few cents, but it will mean so much to the Junior who is just learning the meaning of ownership. The Bible should be chosen to fit the size of the Junior.

In churches that conduct confirmation courses, Bibles are usually presented by the church on Confirmation Sunday. Often such Bibles are *as good as new* after ten or twenty years; they have never been used. Some churches now present the Bibles when the pupils enroll. Thus the Bibles are used and marked during the course. This ties lesson experience with the book itself. It becomes a conditioning to the Bible. In some churches that sponsor a two year confirmation course, the Bibles are presented to the first year student on the evening of the Sunday when the second year students graduate. This is a very practical plan. The graduates receive their certificates, while next year's class receive their Bibles.

Adults, too, are in need of Biblical instruction. Their knowledge of the contents of the Bible is painfully meager even though they may have been active church members for several years. The author of the epistle to the Hebrews refers to immature Christians as being bottle fed babies in Christ. They remained on a religious milk diet when they should be sinking their teeth into theological steaks (cf. Hebrews 5:12-14; note also I Corinthians 3:1-3). We have in our churches of today many adults to whom the pastor must serve a sermonic milk diet. Educationally they have remained in the ecclesiastical kindergarten too long. Teaching the Bible to adults becomes one of the pastor's many responsibilities. Midweek services have in many churches been revitalized by combining definite Bible study with the traditional prayer and testimony midweek meetings.

Church History

There are devout Christians who are well informed about the history of the Hebrew people as recorded in the Bible, but who are woefully ignorant as to the experiences of the Christian church during the centuries between the time the new Testament was first compiled and our present time. They seem to think that God was very active in Biblical times, but that he went on a prolonged vacation at the close of the first century and then became active again at the time of the Protestant reformation. Church history as taught in the average theological seminary is often very factual and often painfully dry — names, dates, church conferences, theological controversies, etc. But need it be? A few years ago I visited the class of a church history professor in an eastern seminary. He made an assignment to his students that impressed me as being extremely practical. It was to prepare a plan to teach Church history to the young people of the churches they would serve. Since I was a visitor for only that one day, I did not have the opportunity to see the finished projects. I have since that often wondered why other teachers of church history do not make similar assignments.

There is also *denominational history*. In our ecumenical age, we are apt to neglect to inform our youth of the history of the denomination to which they belong. A college freshman was asked in class *why* she belonged to a certain denomination. She answered "My father! When I was a small girl I wanted to be a Methodist, but my father wouldn't let me." This was a very frank answer. A little probing revealed the fact that she did not have the slightest idea of how her *father's* church differed from the Methodists. Our youth should be able to give a reason for their faith, even to the extent of why they are Baptists, Episcopalians, Lutherans, Methodists, Presbyterians or some other denomination. Such information need not make them clannish or ecclesiastical isolationists; they should know in a general way what their church believes. This is a part of Christian culture.

Worship

We often hear the complaint that modern youth lacks reverence. One reason is that we have never seriously tried to teach them the spirit and techniques of group worship. Another reason is that we older Christians have not set a good example in our worship. We have ourselves either not known how to worship; or if we once knew, we have forgotten. Unless we teach our youth the great hymns of the church, we should not be surprised if we discover that they have developed a taste for religious flippancy set to jazz rhythm. The pastor will find it extremely difficult to create an atmosphere of worship on Sunday morning if the "worshipers" have been brought up through the Sunday School with religious pep rallies, and gospel syncopation. Worship, some claim, is a certain mood that is caught rather than taught. But much can be done to create the type of environment that is conducive to the mood of worship. We must teach our youth *how* to worship.

Stewardship

Stewardship is attitude as well as act. Legalistically to pay one's tenth to the Lord as a sense of duty may enrich the church's coffers, but it is more in the spirit of Mosaic law than Christian liberty. The child who asks his father each Sunday for a penny to give in the Sunday School collection is neither learning the value of money nor the meaning of stewardship. We need to teach a threefold stewardship; *talents, time,* and *tithing.* Often we think of stewardship only in terms of dollars and cents, forgetting that our time and our talents belong to God just as much as our material possessions.

Christian Citizenship

An English clergyman, Guy H. King, has published an exposition of the epistle of James giving the book the striking title, *A Belief That Behaves.* Being a Christian in the twentieth century is more than adopting a system of religious thought and cultivating attitudes; it is behavior as well. James stresses that faith without works is dead (James 2:17). In the book of Acts, we find the disciples referred to as those of the *way* (9:2; 19:9; 22:4; 24:14, 22). It was a way of living. They had found not *a* way, but *the* way.

To tell our youth to be good and to *behave* themselves is meaningless unless we spell out the good behavior in terms of deeds. Youthful energy and enthusiasm needs to be channeled. Christian education should provide such channels. The philosophy proposed by some that neither parents nor teachers should interfere in curbing or directing the natural human urges, but let youth find out for themselves what is morally right and wrong, can only lead to confusion. There is conduct which is pleasing to God, and behavior which dishonors Him. We want our children to behave as civilized human beings in social settings, so we teach them how they are to conduct themselves; we stress table manners for we do not want our children to eat like animals. Without forming iron bound molds of conduct, a regimented behavior, it is our responsibility to present Christian behavior patterns that may serve as general directives, recognizing individual differences even in Christian conduct.

Christian citizenship is not a mere matter of obeying the laws of the community and country and going to the polls to cast one's ballot on election day. Even children share in citizenship through their conduct at home, in school, on the playground, and in church. It is the responsibility of the church to teach Christian citizenship to children and adults alike. *What is the pastor's part in this educational program?*

That is the topic for our subsequent discussion. As administrative head of the local church, he is responsible for all of the activities sponsored by his church. Even in a small church, he will discover before long that if he tries to do it all himself, he will be spreading out his services so thin that his entire ministry becomes superficial. He must decide what aspects of his ministry he can and should delegate to others and what he must undertake himself. The old saying that it is better to get ten men to do a piece of work than to do ten men's work yourself is especially true of the pastor of the local church. But to what extent is the average pastor qualified to direct the educational ministry of the local church? In the next chapter, we shall consider his preparation for this responsibility.

Suggested readings

Gaebelein, Frank E., *Christian Education in a Democracy*, Oxford, 1951
Mason, Harold C., *Abiding Values in Christian Education*, Revell, 1955
Miller, Randolph Crump, *The Clue to Christian Education*, Scribner's, 1950
Murch, James DeForest, *Christian Education and the Local Church*, Standard Publishing, Revised 1958
Sherrill, Lewis J., *Family and Church*, Abingdon, 1937
Smart, James D., *The Teaching Ministry of the Church*, Westminster, 1954
Smith, Rockwell C., *The Church in our Town*, Abingdon-Cokesbury, 1945
Vieth, Paul H., *The Church and Christian Education*, Bethany, 1946

Topics for further thought

1. How does the Roman Catholic church differ from the Evangelical Christian church in its methods of communicating the gospel?

2. What are the advantages and disadvantages of the use of mass media in propagating the gospel?

3. What are the basic reasons for the recent resurgence of interest in the *teaching* ministry of the Protestant church?

4. What are the psychological differences between *preaching* and *teaching?*

5. To what extent should theology be introduced into the Sunday School curricula?

2

The Minister as Educator

Most churches choose their pastors according to evaluation of pulpit performance. It is still the practice in many churches to invite the candidate to occupy the pulpit on some Sunday to deliver a *sample sermon*. Attempts to abolish this traditional practice have not been altogether effective; hence, the policy survives. Pastors generally do not favor this public spectacle. An otherwise *good* preacher may under the stress of the situation fail to make a favorable impression upon his critical audience. Then, too, a candidate anxious to elicit a call may yield to the temptation of "plowing with another man's heifer" and memorize a classic sermon prepared and preached by some great pulpit orator and then deliver it, forgetting or neglecting the quotation marks. Or the candidate may become so inspired in facing a new and large audience that he soars far above his average Sunday preaching. Even if the congregation were seeking a pulpiteer rather than a pastor, the one sermon sample is not a wise guide for selecting one who Sunday after Sunday is to stand in the pulpit to deliver the gospel goods.

But the pastor must be more than a preacher, however important that is. He must function as an administrator, social worker, public relations person, counselor, and teacher as well. He needs to be more than a teacher; he should be an educator. The teacher should know *what* to do; the educator should know the *why*. The former may be achieved through coaching but the latter requires a general understanding of the basic principles and philosophies that undergird the programs and practices of learning. That does not mean that the pastor in order to function as an educator must, besides his theological training, also have a graduate degree in education; but it does mean that he should have had in his training for the ministry something more than a *required* one semester course in Christian education wedged into the curriculum wherever two or three hours may be reserved.

The graduate of the twentieth century theological seminary is well prepared to preach, but the average Protestant pastor performs in the pulpit only once or twice one day of the week whereas his educational responsibilities should be distributed through the seven days.

As educational counselor

First of all in his own family as his children enter and continue in the public school, he should understand and appreciate what the public school is trying to do for his children. He needs to give wise counsel to his own children in order that they may derive full benefit from the educational opportunities the state offers them. When they arrive at the high school level, there is the vocational guidance as well as the choice of college to continue their education. The modern high school offers professional guidance in making such choices, but parents can not afford to have these vital matters decided by "outsiders." The pastor should be able intelligently to cooperate with professionally trained counselors in helping the youth find their place in society.

Then, too, the pastor may become the educational counselor of families in his parish. Perplexed parents come to him with their educational as well as spiritual problems. It may be Johnny's poor grades and aversion to the elementary school, or it may be Mary's determination to get a job rather than going on to college after graduation from high school. The pastor may be just as confused as the parents, but he should be willing to listen attentively as they project their problems.

Adolescents generally are less prone to listen to the counsel of parents than they are to talk matters over with their pastor. Often the pastor comes to find himself a mediator. The pastor who has an appreciation of educational problems may be able to discuss with both parents and youth without seeming to be either evasive or dogmatic.

In Parent-Teacher Associations, the pastor may wield a wholesome influence. The very fact that he attends the meetings is evidence of his interest. His presence is felt even when he has no part in the program. It is not enough that his wife is active in the PTA; he himself should be representing his own family as well as his church. There is no good reason why the pastor should not be a member, as well as the florist, the druggist, or the mechanic.

As a teacher

Many pastors teach adult Bible classes in the Sunday School. Often these classes become preaching services, the "students" being passive listeners, their only active participation being that of contributing a coin, or perchance a dollar bill to the class collection. The result has often been that the members of the Bible class have absented themselves from the regular church worship service. They have been *preached at* once; why be preached at a second time so soon? The problem of the pastor and the Sunday School will be discussed in a later chapter.

Since later chapters will be devoted to confirmation classes, Vacation Church Schools, Weekday Church Schools and leadership training, we shall not discuss them at present except to state that they offer the pastor opportunities for contributing towards Christian education.

As participant at special educational occasions

The baccalaureate speaker at high school commencements is usually one of the local pastors. He need offer no apologies for giving a gospel message, but it should be different from the traditional Sunday morning sermon. If he has familiarity with education, he may challenge faculty and graduates alike by presenting the gospel within an educational framework. In college communities, local pastors are often called upon to share in the chapel services. There are in general three types of chapel talks presented by pastors. First there is the "warmed over" Sunday sermon. It may have been very good when delivered fresh on Sunday morning, but be rather stale when given in the college chapel on Monday. Then there is the chapel speaker who wants to be popular through entertaining his audience. His "talk" consists of a parade of stories, some funny, some "chestnuts," some juvenile, and some even bordering on the risque, with perhaps a melodramatic sob story to conclude the "message." But there is also the pastor who comes to the chapel service with a definite spiritual objective. He understands the adolescent or young adult, his needs and his interests. He avoids confusing theological terminology, and presents the challenge of Christ in terms college youth can understand. The student body leaves the chapel service having received inspiration as well as food for thought. There is a large field for educational evangelism among the youth enrolled in our Christian colleges.

As an alumnus, the pastor may be invited to his Alma Mater as commencement speaker. His address need not be a discourse on education, but it should have educational implications. The address needs to be more integrated than a sermon spiced with quotations from modern educators. Unless the speaker's own mind has been steeped in educational thought, his quotations will seem strangely artificial.

A pastor who can speak intelligently about educational matters whether in public or in private conversation adds community prestige to the church he serves as well as gains respect for himself from the educational forces in his parish.

The average pastor is poorly equipped for the teaching ministry

The standard American theological seminary prescribes three years of graduate work as a prerequisite for graduation. In order to enroll in the seminary, the candidate must have had four years of undergraduate studies with a bachelor's degree in the liberal arts. The attempt to conserve the traditional seminary courses while adding new ones has resulted in a crowded curriculum. Some seminaries have seriously considered adding a fourth year in order to make room for the new courses. Several seminaries already require four years of work for graduation, one year consisting of field work serving either as assistant pastors or as pastors of some of the smaller churches. The suggestion has been made that perhaps we are trying to offer too many courses.

Some could be included as units in some other course. It is a suggestion well worth considering.

Examining the catalogs of ten of our leading seminaries, we find that some have several courses in religious education listed but only one or two semester courses are required for graduation. The number of required courses is so large that it is quite difficult to fit in desirable electives. As a result, courses in Christian education become incidental or perhaps a senior year postscript. To require a three-hour one-semester course of seminary seniors who have had no previous training in educational procedure can scarcely be called preparation for the teaching ministry. At best it can be but a hurried survey of the field. Graduates from Missionary training schools and Bible institutes are better equipped for teaching than are most graduates of our theological seminaries. Most seminary deans are aware of this neglect. But the problem is, what can we omit from the present curriculum in order to give room for additional courses in education?

The Christian college should stress courses in education

The pre-theological college courses advocated by some seminaries have proved more idealistic than practical. If the ministerial candidates were recruited from the high schools, their college courses could be selected so as to prepare them for entrance into the seminary. But many come from state colleges and universities where no courses in religion are offered. Then, too, many have not decided upon the ministry as their vocation before they were college seniors.

The Christian college should have a strong department of Christian education with enough courses to make possible majors and minors. The average Christian college is so anxious to imitate state schools that it often forgets its Christian character. If church sponsored colleges are to be worthy of the church members' support, they must dispense education with a plus. They must provide opportunities for its students to have personal vital Christian experiences, to develop mature Christian personalities, and to prepare for service to the community, the church, and the country. This calls for courses in content as well as in methods of service. The college freshmen should all be required to take a survey course in English Bible. These courses should be more than Sunday School classes taught on weekdays. On the other hand they should not be seminary courses presenting problems of Biblical criticism that would tend to confuse rather than clarify. Well meaning teachers are sometimes guilty of irreparable harm in teaching such Bible courses to college freshmen. The childhood faith of the student is not only shaken but torn up without the rebuilding of a more mature faith. There are critical problems that should be seriously considered in the theological seminary when the student's mental maturity as well as his integrated general religious knowledge makes it possible to think things through. There are things we can teach with understanding to high school seniors that would only confuse the third grader in the elementary school.

Without attempting to prescribe a curriculum, we would propose a sequence of courses in Christian education beyond the freshman year. Sophomores would profit from a one semester course in basic Christian doctrines and a second semester of Christian ethics. For the juniors it might be well to have a one semester course in *Introduction to Christian Education* and a second semester on *Methods of Christian Education*. During the senior year the student may be permitted to choose from several electives in the field of religion. The student who after college graduation enrolls in the seminary then has a good background in Christian education. The student who chooses some other vocation may render valuable service as a lay worker in some local church. In either case the church receives returns for its educational investments.

Masters' degrees in education in theological seminaries

Complying with a request from both ministerial students and local churches for further training in Christian education some seminaries are offering a Master's degree to students who continue their studies for a year beyond earning their Bachelor of Divinity degrees.

From the foregoing, it is evident that the average pastor is

professionally poorly prepared for directing the important teaching ministry of the local church. But he need not despair.
Through self-directed study he may become well informed in
the field of Christian education. He should subscribe to some
Christian educational journal and study each issue carefully.
There are excellent stimulating books available. The pastor will
want to add a few such books to his personal library. A couple
of hours each week devoted to the thoughtful reading of such
books will prove to be a good educational investment. A book
on Christian education provides good vacation time reading.
Check with the publishers of your own denomination to learn
what materials in this field they have published. Most pastors
are not familiar with the literary and educational products of
their own denomination. But do not become clannish. Read
books published by other denominations and interdenominational publishers as well. You may blame the seminary where
you trained for neglecting to train you for the teaching ministry, but you have only yourself to blame if you *remain* ignorant.

Suggested readings

Blackwood, Andrew, *Pastoral Leadership*, Abingdon-Cokesbury, 1949
Bushnell, Horace, *Christian Nurture*, Yale University, revised 1947
Eakin, Mildred Moody and Frank, *The Pastor and Children*, Macmillan Co.,
    1947
Hensley, J. Clark, *The Pastor as Educational Director*, Central Seminary
    Press, 1946
Lindhorst, Frank A., *The Minister Teaches Religion*, Abingdon, 1945
Mason, Harold C., *Abiding Values in Christian Education*, Chapter 6, Revell,
    1955
Munro, Harry C., *The Pastor and Religious Education*, Abingdon, 1930
Murch, James DeForest, *Christian Education and the Local Church*, Chap-
    ter 20, Standard Publishing, Revised, 1958

Topics for further thought

1. What required courses could be omitted from the seminary curriculum in order to make room for more Christian education courses?

2. What would be the advantages and disadvantages of adding another
year to the seminary training?

3. If only one course is required in Christian education, should it be
given the first, second, or third year? Why?

4. How could a congregation ascertain a candidate's ability for the teaching ministry of the church?

5. Under what circumstances might a pastor become so interested in the
teaching ministry that he neglects his other pastoral responsibilities?

3
The Local Church Organized for Teaching

Modern man lives in a highly organized society. There are associations, brotherhoods, clubs, fraternities, societies, unions, etc. Although less complex, primitive man finds his life largely controlled by tribal and clan rules, regulations and taboos. It is quite evident that the first century church was organized and administered. The book of Acts and the Pauline epistles reflect church government. But organization is not an end in itself but a means to an end. The purpose of organization is two-fold, first to facilitate the functioning of each unit, and second, to coordinate the different functional agencies.

Most modern churches are over organized. They have too many, and too complicated organizations. To use an antiquated analogy, "there is too much harness for too little horse." Churches with a membership of less than a hundred have organizations more than adequate for a church with a membership five times as large. Many churches have developed organizational machinery that is so elaborate that they have neither the spiritual power nor the personnel to operate. They resemble Ezekiel's vision of wheels within wheels (Ezekiel 1:15-21). Note, however, that in Ezekiel's vision "a living Spirit was in these wheels" (Moffatt). Ezekiel presents another warning regarding organization without life in his vision of the valley of dry bones (37:1-10). The bones were "very dry"; they lacked life.

Church organizations come into being for two reasons: first a felt need, and second, imitation of some other church. The ordaining of the seven "to serve tables" while the twelve would devote themselves to "prayer and to the ministry of the word" did not come as the result of a vision or a dream. The complaint of negligence in the distribution of the necessities of life led the *twelve* to summon the *body of the disciples* (the church). Of the seven chosen two became lay preachers — Stephen and Philip. In the later epistles several church officers are mentioned, elders, deacons, bishops, etc. Organizations sometimes survive for sentimental reasons even after the need is no longer evident. Small churches often imitate the larger churches in their organizational patterns. As a result of such carbon copy procedure the small church tries to fit new "wheels" into the church machinery even where they become a burden rather than a boon.

Some basic principles of church organization

Denominations differ as to their organizational patterns, and churches within the same denomination differ in some details. There are, however, a few basic principles that should guide whatever the patterns may be.

1. The pastor is the head of the local church as Christ is the head of the universal church. He is not the errand boy of the congregation; he is the shepherd of his flock. He is exofficio a member of all boards.

2. Each organization should have specific objectives, goals to meet some specific needs. These should be clearly defined.

3. The function of these organizations should be directed and supervised by duly elected boards, and directors called by the church.

4. The boards shall consist of members of the local church.

5. The function of the different boards shall be coordinated in an executive board of the church.

6. These boards are responsible to the congregation and should at specified times give a report of their activities to the membership in general.

7. Each board may adopt specific rules for the conduct of its affairs but all matters of policies must be submitted to the congregation for approval.

The board of Christian education

We are in this study not concerned with the other boards

of the church except as they relate to the teaching ministry. Some churches have committees on Christian education, but a committee has no executive power; it can recommend but it can not act. A *board* on the other hand has the authority to act within the limits of its own sphere. The titles differ; some call it the board of *parish* education, others *board of education,* still others board of *Christian* education. It is the function rather than the name that is significant. The board may consist of three, six, or nine members, depending upon the size of the church. A three year term is suggested, with members elected in such manner that there will always be a carry over of some member, or members, each year. Then after the first term there will never be an altogether new board. There will always be carry overs, insuring continuity of board policies and projects.

Some churches include the pastor and Sunday School superintendent as regular members of the board, even naming one of them as chairman. This may not be a wise policy, the pastor is by virtue of his office an exofficio member of all boards. Neither the superintendent nor the director of Christian education should be voting members of the board. The function of the board is to supervise their work. There may be times when the board will want to meet without these persons present when they wish to critically evaluate their leadership. The pastor, however, should if possible be present at every meeting of the board.

The tradition of annually electing the superintendent by the popular vote of the congregation may be a good democratic policy but it is poor educational procedure. The board should carefully select *one* candidate for the office and present that name to the congregation for approval. Presenting two candidates may be democratic but psychologically it is not the best policy. In Christian education we should refrain from playing politics.

The superintendent too should be granted a term of office ... three, four, or five years ... with the possibility of re-election to a second term. With a term of office before him, the newly elected superintendent may in consultation with his staff make plans, covering several years, to be presented to and approved by the board, these may be annual goals connected in a sequence.

Some pastors consider the board of Christian education as being concerned only with the teaching of children, but its field should extend to all teaching agencies of the church whether dealing with children or adults. Besides the Sunday School this should include Vacation Church Schools, Weekday Church Schools, confirmation classes, youth work, and adult education.

The board should evaluate and approve all curricula used in the church's teaching ministry. At the recommendation of the superintendent and director of Christian education, the board shall consider the choice of all teachers and counselors.

Proposed pattern for church organization

A All officials called or elected by the church
B trustees
C diaconate
D board of Christian Education

The pastor is exofficio member of all boards. In some churches the diaconate is divided into *deacons* and *deaconesses*.

In order to work effectively, the board of Christian education must be given the same status as the other boards of the church. It must be more than a mere appendage to some other board. The plan of organization we submit has the advantage that it is applicable to either large or small churches. In order to function effectively the boards should meet monthly, likewise all the boards should meet together as a church board once a month in order to hear reports from the respective boards. At the annual meeting of the congregation, officers and board members are elected, budgets are presented and policies are discussed and determined. The plan is democratic yet coordinated and directed.

Administering the educational program

A machine, no matter how carefully built, will not function without power. So also human organizations whether they be political, social, or ecclesiastical must have personnel in order to be effective. Even the best of machines equipped with power function poorly if operated by ignorant or careless persons. It is possible to have adequate equipment and a perfect plan for teaching — on paper — and yet fail to produce the desired results because of poor administration and inferior teachers. Administration may become a hindrance rather than a help when the administrator becomes dominant. It was Thomas Jefferson who said "that government is best that governs least." Pastors are sometimes tempted to think of themselves administratively as *supermen*. They want to *run* everything. Chairmen of the different boards are afraid to exert themselves out of fear of the superman. The democratic church becomes an absolute monarchy with the pastor as czar. Those who are supposed to be leaders in their boards and offices lose interest and initiative. They operate like puppets with the pastor manipulating the strings. Brethren, these things should not be so!

As a country lad in my late teens, I was given some sound advice from a kind and wise neighbor. I had taken a four-week summer course in the operation of steam engine. I had even received a certificate stating that I was qualified to operate such machines. True, I had many pages of theory in my notebooks, but I was aware of the fact that I lacked practical experience.

Learning that I was about to get my experience as "engineer" of a large steam tractor the good neighbor gave me this bit of advice. "Some people think that in order to be a good engineer one must go around with a wrench in his hand tightening a nut here and loosening one there. As long as your engine runs, leave it alone. Use the oil can instead of a wrench." Wise words! In administering church organizations, there is a temptation to use the wrench instead of the oil can. Organizational friction is reduced by the application of a little oil of human understanding. When tempted to reach for the wrench to change things, reach for the oil can instead. "A soft answer turneth away wrath but a grievous word stirreth up anger" (Proverbs 15:1). Even in the Christian church there is personality friction; it becomes the pastor's responsibility to reduce this friction to a minimum. A well adjusted machine operates quietly; so does also a well adjusted church board.

Varieties in local church organizations

William James in 1902 published a book that has become a classic, *The Varieties of Religious Experience*. A few years ago Sverre Norborg published a book with a similar title, *Varieties of Christian Experience*. The primary difference is that the one uses the word *Religious* while the other uses *Christian*. Both emphasize individual differences. Since there are differences in the individuals' religious experiences, we are not surprised that there are also differences in patterns of organization. Some denominations are based on broad democratic principles which are reflected in the autonomy of the local church while others have a centralized type of government. One can not say that the one pattern is superior to the other. The important thing is not the pattern but the products of the organization.

The purpose of this chapter is not to sell a prepared blue print, but to call the pastor's attention to the need of some type of organization and administration in the local church that shall facilitate the teaching ministry. We would suggest that the pastor secure from the publishers of his denomination pamphlets on the setting up of boards of parish education, Christian education, or by whatever name such boards are known. In some denominations their national boards of education have prepared printed or mimeographed suggestions. It may be well to learn what other denominations are doing also. A cross fertilization of denominational policies and practices is usually productive of new ideas.

We would conclude with a word of admonition, do not become a slave to *ecclesiastical machinery*. There is nothing sacred about organization no matter how deep the traditional roots. Organizations should not be firmly fixed like the ancient laws of the Medes and Persians. They should be rigid enough to guide but flexible enough to adjust to new situations.

Suggested readings

Benson, Clarence, *The Sunday School in Action*, Moody Press, Revised 1941

Cummings, Oliver D., *Christian Education in the Local Church*, Judson, 1942

Lobinger, John Leslie, *The Better Church School*, Pilgrim, 1952

Mason, Harold C., *Abiding Values in Christian Education*, Chapter X, Revell, 1955

Miller, Randolph Crump, *Education for Christian Living*, Part IV, Prentice Hall, 1956

Murch, James DeForest, *Christian Education and the Local Church*, Chapters 19-23, Standard Publishing, Revised 1958

Smith, Rockwell C., *Rural Church Administration*, Abingdon, 1953

Smith, Irene, *Solving Church School Problems*, Warner, 1944

Stout, John E., *Organization and Administration of Religious Education*, Abingdon, 1922

Topics for further thought

1. What should be the qualifications of members of a board of Christian education in a local church?

2. What are the differences in purpose and administrative authority of the following: *committee, commission, council,* and *board* as they pertain to the educational work of the church?

3. Should the pastor have *veto power* over the decisions of boards?

4. If the church has a full time director of education, should there also be a Sunday School superintendent?

5. If you were to reorganize your church, what changes would you suggest that would affect the teaching ministry?

Age Levels in Christian Education

The pastor of the local church is called to be the shepherd of all ages within his parish, from the playful lambs to the butting rams. His responsibility is not limited to leading his flock to the green pastures and beside the still waters. He is to seek the lost and to prevent the lambs from straying. When Christ commissioned the penitent Peter, he charged him not only to "tend my sheep" and "feed my sheep" but the first command was to "feed my lambs" (John 21:15, 16). Some pastors have a special concern for the children of the church while others are annoyed by them. They would prefer that God would create human beings full grown as he did Adam. To them an ideal church would consist only of intellectual adults capable of appreciating sermonic solid food. There are a few "down town" churches that minister only to adults, but they can scarcely be called either typical or ideal.

An increasing number of pastors are coming to recognize the importance of the child in the *midst* of the group of disciples. With the neighbors of Zacharias, Elizabeth, and baby John, they are seriously asking, "What is this child's future going to be?" (Luke 1:66, Phillips). Nearly two centuries ago John Wesley commanded the preachers of the Methodist society to spend at least one hour twice a week instructing the children. If they were not willing to do this, he considered them unworthy of being Methodist ministers. Pastors who can not become actively interested in children and adolescent youth are to be pitied rather than blamed. They are lacking in qualities that are essential to an effective pastoral ministry.

For practical purposes the average life span, like ancient Gaul, may be divided into three parts, childhood, adolescence and adulthood. Childhood is usually considered to cover the years from birth to twelve years of age, adolescence from twelve to twenty-five, and adulthood from adolescence on. This we grant is not a scientifically refined classification, but it does help to point out differences in needs and interests based on age. Besides difference in age, there are other factors such as racial traits, native capacity for learning, family background, etc. These are all significant, but since we are dealing with this problem in one *chapter* instead of in a whole *book*, we must refer to them only in passing. The difference in native intelligence is a serious educational problem. At one end of the scale, we have the idiot, at the other end, the genius. The idiot and imbecile are usually provided with custodial care in some institution, but the moron is the responsibility of the home and the church. Such feeble minded persons have poor heads but often good hearts. They are in great need of wise guidance lest they become the prey of vicious leadership and become involved in anti-social acts, or even crime. The common practice of grouping children in Sunday School exclusively in terms of age may mean that a teacher finds herself with a moron and a genius in the same class. How to mediate Christian education to both extremes constitutes a serious pedagogical problem.

The fact that three generations sleep under the same roof and eat at the same table does not mean that they constitute a homogeneous group. Grandparents, and grandchildren may be at opposite poles of thought and interests, but they must find some common ground of coexistence. Modern Christian education has been guilty of dividing and subdividing our churches and our families until we have become as strangers to one another. We must strive for unity without uniformity, a recognition of graded instruction without departmental isolation.

Childhood

The apostle Paul recognizes age levels in speech, thought, and emotions (I Corinthians 13:11). He accuses the members of the Corinthian church of behaving like children. "Quit you like men" (I Corinthians 16:13). This is not a reflection upon childhood but a censure of adults who had developed physically but had failed to mature intellectually, morally, and emotionally.

Entering the public school at the age of six is a psychological rather than physiological division of childhood. The time from birth to six years of age is usually referred to as the *pre-school* period. This does not mean that the child's education *begins* when he enrolls in the first grade. His education began the day he was born. There are no formal lessons, no textbooks, no class schedules, but the pre-school child learns. He imitates, he imagines, he inquires. The foundations for his moral behavior are laid long before he comes under the influence of the formal school. He has inherited a capacity for learning but he has not inherited an education. All his information must be acquired first hand. He reacts to anything and everything in his immediate environment. The pastor's recognition of the child by a smile and a friendly handshake means more than a similar gesture to an adult. The modern Sunday School makes the kindergarten as much like home to the child as possible, with rugs on the floor, pictures on the wall, and even toys. The teacher is usually a motherly type of individual. Even though the pastor does not have a child of his own in this age group, he should occasionally visit the department in order to encourage the teachers as well as to become identified as the shepherd of the lambs, so the child may come to feel "he is my pastor."

When the six year old is enrolled in the first grade of the elementary school, he finds himself in a strange situation. Another woman, the teacher, supplants his mother. He is no longer free to do what he pleases whenever he pleases. As an infant he was fenced in by his play pen; now he is fenced in by the four walls of his classroom. The kindergarten, both in Sunday School and in the public school, has partly prepared him for this curtailment of his freedom. The primary child (grades 1-3) is only learning to read. His major learning is thus not from the textbook but from the teacher's personality and the social impact of his school mates. He learns both mischief and good behavior for he is an imitator. The first three years in the elementary school helps him to become orientated, he is gradually becoming a person.

The *junior* is an animated unit of humanity. He cannot sit perfectly still, not even in church. His muscles throb for action. The educational problem is not to thwart these natural urges but to direct them into worthwhile channels of activity. The pastor should not become impatient with the junior's restlessness in the Sunday morning service. There may be adults in the audience who feel the same way but who can control their muscles even when the nerves become jittery. The pastor who gains the confidence of the *junior* has paved the way for continued confidence when the junior becomes an intermediate. Most adolescent problems have their roots in the pre-adolescent period. In the church's effort to minister to its *teenagers,* she is in danger of neglecting the junior. It is one of the pastor's many responsibilities to guard against such neglect.

Adolescence

The much used term *teenager* is a popular rather than an educational expression. *Adolescence* is a more scientific term and includes the years from twelve to twenty-five. It is a period of growing into adulthood. Psychologists group the adolescent into three age levels, *early* adolescents (12, 13, 14), *middle* adolescents (15, 16, 17), and *later* adolescents (18-25). Educationally they are classified as junior high, senior high, and college. The traditional Sunday School departmentalizes them as intermediates (12, 13, 14), seniors (15, 16, 17), youth (18-25). The range of interests and needs within the age group of adolescents becomes evident when we compare a thirteen year old boy in the junior high school with the graduate university student who at twenty-five years of age is about to receive his Ph.D. degree. They have very little in common except the fact that they are moving along on the same American educational assembly line.

Graduation from high school means more than receiving a diploma. It brings the adolescent to the crossroads where certain decisions must be made. What vocation shall he choose? Shall he go on to college or get a job? Family ties are loosened and often broken. For eighteen years the parents have given guidance, provided food, clothing and lodging. Now the adolescent is on his own. Even if he continues to live at home his status has changed. Leaving home means leaving the church of one's childhood. Many students who lose their religion in college never had a personal religion to lose. It was the religion of the family or the church, but not one that he could really call his own. The pastor who has given direction through preaching, teaching, and counseling to his young people during the high school years has contributed much, not in providing them with a ready made faith, but in helping them to tailor a faith that meets both their needs and interests. In a later chapter, we shall consider the pastor's responsibility to the youth of college age.

The high school years are important from the point of view of the educational ministry of the church. This is the age when large numbers stray from the church. Then, too, in many parishes, there is a great exodus after high school graduation as youth transfer to other cities for study or work. In many rural churches very few young people remain in the home community after high school. The *youth work* of necessity becomes limited to the high school age.

Adulthood

Formerly it was customary to classify all grown ups as *adults*. Recently we have come to discover differences that would warrant a threefold grouping. Earl Ziegler refers to them as *Beginning Adulthood* (Young Adults), *Continuing Adulthood* (Middle aged), and *Arriving Adults* (Older People).

Of the young adult, Ralph Sockman says that it is the *dangerous* age. Robert Havighurst says of them, "Of all the periods of life, early adulthood is the fullest of teachable moments and the emptiest of efforts to teach." As churches we have been so concerned about preparing activity programs and giving guidance to adolescents that we have forgotten, or perhaps not stopped to realize, that those just entering upon the responsibilities of adulthood are in need of guidance and instruction also. There are delinquent families as well as individuals within this age bracket.

The average pastor beams his ministry largely to the "continuing adults." They constitute the pillars of the church. It is they who support the work of the church financially. They have the "say so" at church business meetings. This is the age group the pastor strives to cultivate even if at times it may mean some weeding. The pastor thinks that he understands both their needs and interests. But often, he mistakes his own interests for those of his adult members. It is misleading to generalize about adults, for there are individual differences that create problems in communicating the gospel whether through preaching or teaching. The alert pastor will focus his attention upon individuals rather than upon the adult group. He must become a gospel retailer rather than wholesaler.

Some individuals grow old earlier than others. Heredity seems to be a factor as well as general health and type of vocation. The age of sixty-five has come to be considered as the dividing line between the *Middle aged* and *Older People,* but for psychological rather than physiological reasons. The current practice of retiring workers at the age of sixty-five regardless of mental or physical health creates emotional problems. Some retired persons deteriorate rapidly both physically and mentally unless there are new interesting activities in which they can engage. They come to feel that they are not needed, perhaps not even wanted. They feel they are burdens on society. Some become cantankerous and bitter while others seem to mellow with the years. These older people respond to education and guidance if wisely administered. This, too, becomes the pastor's educational responsibility. Whether these retired saints shall become an asset or a liability to the local church is an educational as well as economic problem.

The pastor whose ambition is to be the good shepherd of the entire flock needs to acquaint himself with the capacities, needs, and interests of the different age levels. He should add at least three books to his personal library, one on child psychology, another on adolescence and the third on the psychology of the adult. Mastering the contents of three such books will help him to understand his own family, even his own self, besides the people of his parish to whom he ministers. He will discover, too, that he will become familiar with the personal traits of Biblical characters. The children, youth, and adults portrayed in the Bible will prove to be very similar to those of the same age groups in our modern times. It opens up new vistas of thought both for preaching and teaching. Human nature is very much the same in the twentieth century of the Christian era as it was twenty centuries before Christ.

Suggested readings

Caldwell, Irene Smith, *Our Concern is Children*, Warner, 1948
Chamberlin, J. Gordon, *The Church and its Young People*, Abingdon, 1943
Gorham, Donald, *Understanding Adults*, Judson, 1948
Havighurst and Albrecht, *Older People*, Longmans, Green, 1953
Jones, Mary Alice, *The Church and the Children*, Cokesbury, 1935
Seidman, Jerome S., *The Adolescent* (readings), Dryden, 1953
Strang, Ruth, *An Introduction to Child Study*, Macmillan, Revised 1951
Wattenberg, William W., *The Adolescent Years*, Harcourt, Brace, 1955
Whitehouse, Elizabeth, *The Children we Teach*, Judson, 1950
Zeigler, Earl F., *Christian Education of Adults*, Westminster, 1958

Topics for further thought

1. Why do scholarly pastors often find it difficult to adjust to different age levels?

2. What can the church do to educate the feeble minded?

3. What is the difference between graded lesson materials and graded methods of teaching?

4. How far is it true that you cannot teach an old dog new tricks?

5. To what extent may a pastor become too conscious of age levels in his parish?

5
The Minister in the Sunday Church School

The American Sunday School is a generally established institution of religious education. Whether the pastor serves a large or a small church, has his parish located in an urban or a rural community, he will have contacts with the Sunday School. The Sunday School is a vital part of the work of the local church. What shall be the pastor's part in its function? There are short sighted pastors who would eliminate the traditional Sunday School, if they could. They consider the primary function of the pastor to be that of preaching sermons from the pulpit and administering the sacraments. They are apparently not aware that pulpit oratory may attract an *audience,* but that an audience is not a congregation. It takes more than preaching to build a congregation. There must also be teaching, pastoral visitation, and counseling. The pastor need not, and should not, neglect his sermon preparation in order to have an active part in the work of the Sunday School. As pastor of the church, he is automatically the pastor of the Sunday School as well, since the school is a part of the church. His ministry within the Sunday School will bring him into contact with the superintendents, the teachers, parents, and pupils. He should be able to give wise counsel. He may or may not teach a class, but he should display an active interest. There are three leaders within the local church whose friendship the pastor needs to cultivate, the Sunday School superintendent, the director of music, and the chairman of the women's organization. They may be of great help or great hindrance to the pastor in his general ministry, depending whether they work with him or against him.

The pastor and the superintendent

There are in general four types of superintendents.

1. There is the *meek and mild* superintendent. He is a timid soul who holds the office largely because he did not have the courage to decline. He is a *good* person, but he should be good for something. A number of years ago I was visiting with an older pastor. We talked shop. In the course of our conversation, I commented about his young assistant: "He seems to be a *good* young man." The pastor bridled, "Yes, that is the trouble. He is *good,* but he ought to be good for something." In the conversation that followed, I learned what he meant by that remark. As far as character was concerned, the young man was beyond reproach; but he lacked initiative. It is not enough that the superintendent is good; he needs to have vision and courage. Some aggressive teachers do more to direct the Sunday School than does the superintendent. If the superintendent is a young person who in addition to his other limitations also suffers from an inferiority complex, the pastor has to help him to gain self confidence. To the timid young Timothy, the Apostle Paul wrote, "Let no man despise thy youth, but be thou an example of the believers" (I Timothy 4:12).

2. Then there is the *high and haughty* superintendent. He never confers with the pastor and rarely with anyone else. He *runs* the show himself. It is *his* Sunday School. He is usually an aggressive person with many ideas. The Sunday School of which he is *boss* is the great event of Sunday; the preaching and worship service of the church is merely a post script. If it happens that the Sunday School attendance is twice as large as the preaching service attendance, he begins to feel that he is more important than the pastor. He has a wealth of enthusiasm and energy. In modern terminology, he is a "live wire." None of his teachers dare oppose him, he reigns over an absolute monarchy, not a democracy. Such a leader may accomplish much good, but he may also be responsible for friction and frustration on the part of his teachers. The pastor often feels helpless in the situation, for the superintendent does not seek the counsel of the pastor. And if the pastor should offer unsolicited advice, it

would be ignored if not spurned. If through tact and prayerful patience the pastor is finally able to gain his confidence, such strong leadership may be directed into more cooperative channels.

3. There is the *superannuated* type. He is usually a man of middle age, or older. For more than twenty years he has been superintendent of that school. He conducts the Sunday School as they did in the "good old days." He has read no books on Christian education, rarely attends a Sunday School conference. Not only has he gotten into a rut, but he keeps the school in that rut; year by year it becomes deeper. No one wants to hurt the feelings of the old saint; he means well; he is not belligerent, only ignorant; in fact, he evidences traits of senility. He considers it his mission to preserve the old, the traditional. If the pastor subtly tries to get him replaced, he may stir up a hornets' nest, for perhaps half of the congregation are his relatives. So for the sake of peace in the church family at the expense of progress nothing is done. If we wait long enough the good Lord may call him home, but some of these superannuated brethren seem to have charmed lives.

If he is nearing some specific milestone in his capacity as superintendent, the twenty-fifth, for instance, the church may plan a social event honoring him for long and faithful, though not altogether effective service, a certificate might be given him together with some appropriate gift. He would be happy, and so would all concerned. The constitution of the congregation should preclude the possibility of "life tenure" in any office in the local church.

4. Finally there is the *good and faithful servant*. He leads but he does not dominate. He has frequent conferences with his pastor. The teaching staff look up to him with respect and confidence. They are not afraid to make suggestions, for they know that they will be heard even though their proposals may not be adopted. He is open minded but not fickle, stable but not dogmatic. In a superintendent of this type the pastor finds an able assistant. Not only does the superintendent welcome suggestions

from the pastor but the pastor can profit by the superintendant's suggestions as to the pastor's ministry.

The Pastor and the adult Bible class

Adult education in the form of Bible classes encourages and inspires the pastor. There are times, however, when the Adult Bible class may present serious problems. When the members of a Men's Bible class become a *political bloc* and begin to determine the policies of the local church, the pastor becomes concerned, for he may sooner or later find himself at the mercy of the class.

In some instances the Bible class is built around the personality of the teacher. It happens in some cases that he is not even a member of the church where he conducts his class. Doctrinally he may differ rather radically with the views held by the pastor, but he has built up a strong following. The theology of the local church may thus become colored more by the teacher of the Bible class than by the pastor's preaching.

There is still another problem even when the pastor is the teacher. The Bible class becomes a substitute for the regular church service. When the members of the class leave the class room, they also leave the church building — they have done their Sunday duty by the church; they have attended one session.

The new pastor may find that the Men's Bible Class is an established tradition. The teacher may have taught the class for many years and he, too, has become a tradition. What attitude shall the new pastor take towards this old situation? Out of courtesy, the class may ask the pastor to become its teacher, but he often senses that it is a courteous gesture rather than a sincere request based upon conviction.

The pastor as the teacher of a class

Whether or not the pastor shall teach a Sunday School class is a matter that he himself must decide. The call to the pastorate of a church does not as a rule specify that besides his other pastoral duties he is to teach a class. In some churches it has become an established practice that the pastor teaches the adult class. It is taken for granted. In other churches, it is the young people's class that is assigned to the pastor, especially if the pastor is also a young person.

Many pastors prefer not to teach a class. Their arguments are valid. It takes just as much time and energy adequately to prepare a lesson to be taught as to prepare a sermon to be preached. If the teaching session precedes the preaching service, the pastor will have spent so much energy in the teaching that he feels fatigued when he enters the pulpit to preach. He feels that he does not have enough energy to be his best both in the class room and in the pulpit. Is it fair to the Sunday morning audience for the pastor to come before them tired and worn? No general rules can be given as to whether or not the pastor should teach a class, and if he does, what class that should be. If the previous pastor has taught a class, it will be a bit difficult for the new pastor to decline. He might ask to be free from teaching responsibilities for a few months while he is becoming acquainted with the church in general and the Sunday School in particular.

The pastor and the curriculum

In the well organized and administered church, the choice of the curriculum is not made by any one person nor is it made by a popular vote of the teachers and officers. It is the responsibility of the Board of Christian Education of the local church. As an ex-officio member of this board, the pastor wields a decided influence. In discussing the matter of choosing a curriculum, the worker in a church commented, "It is usually what the pastor recommends that is chosen." That pastor had served the church for a number of years and wielded an influence that determined the curriculum. In many churches the curriculum is like the traditional "crazy quilt," a patchwork made up of units from a number of curricula. To many this seems to be ideal — taking the best from several. But unfortunately the result is that the Biblical instruction becomes fragmentary. Some areas of the Bible are sadly neglected while others are covered several times. It is not "rightly dividing the word of truth" (II Timothy 2:15) . Although the pastor is the head of the church, he soon discovers that his lordship over the teaching staff is limited. A few years ago when one of our larger denominations had produced a new graded curriculum for the Sunday School, the teachers of a certain church went on a strike as a protest against the pastor's and superintendent's attempt to coerce them into using the new curriculum of their denomination. The choice of curricula must be a matter of tactful education rather than authoritative legislation.

The pastor as spiritual counselor to the staff

Sunday School teachers need spiritual guidance. While they are seriously striving to give spiritual direction to the lives of their pupils they themselves are in sore need of spiritual orientation. The pastor should be one to whom the confused teacher can come for guidance. He should be familiar enough with abnormal psychology so that he may recognize symptoms of sick personalities that require the help of a doctor of medicine, or even a psychiatrist. There are perhaps more neurotic Sunday School teachers than we realize, and such teachers do their pupils more harm than good. There are so many strange doctrines currently projected in print, on the radio, and television that there is grave danger that even church workers be led astray. The teachers should be encouraged to bring their problems to the pastor. Much of modern neurosis on the part of Christian workers could be prevented if their moral and spiritual problems could be shared with some human being in whom they had confidence. The pastor will need to add some practical books on personal counseling to his library.

The pastor as an occasional visitor

Some pastors who do not teach classes plan to visit some department every Sunday. They may give a brief greeting at the worship service. In schools where each department worships apart from other departments, this seems to be a practical way for the pastor to get around. The departmental superintendent should be informed of the intended visit so that the pastor does not come as a thief in the night. For the pastor to visit a class and sit through a whole session is scarcely fair to the teacher who may become very self-conscious and even resent his visit interpreting it to be a case of "snoopervision" rather than as intended, a friendly visit.

The pastor as superintendent

Under ordinary circumstances, the pastor should not hold the office of superintendent. But there are exceptions to all rules. When a church is being planted in a new community, it may be necessary for the pastor to take the initiative in organizing the Sunday School. There may be no one capable, or willing to assume the leadership of the school, but there may be those who are willing to cooperate as teachers and officers if the pastor will take the lead. In such circumstances, it may be necessary for the pastor to serve as superintendent, but only on a *temporary* basis. After the work gets under way, he may discover some one who is willing to serve as assistant superintendent. With tactful guidance he may soon be both able and willing to assume the leadership.

The future of the local church is invested in the Sunday School of the present. It is, therefore, the pastor's responsibility to promote the project in every way that he can and at the same time guard against developing it to the extent that it becomes a church within the church.

Suggested readings

Athearn, Walter, *The Minister and the Teacher,* Century, 1932

Bonnell, John, *Psychology for Pastor and People,* Harper, 1948

Dicks, Rallo, *Pastoral Work and Personal Counseling,* Macmillan, 1944

Heim, Ralph, *Leading a Sunday Church School,* Muhlenberg, 1950

Hiltner, Seward, *Pastoral Counseling,* Abingdon, 1949

Jones, Philip, *The Church School Superintendent,* Abingdon, 1939

May, Rollo, *The Art of Counseling,* Abingdon, 1939

Miller, Randolph Crump, *A Guide to Church School Teachers,* Seabury, 1947

Vieth, Paul H., *Improving Your Sunday School,* Westminster, 1930; *The Church School,* Christian Education Press, 1957

Topics for further thought

1. What are the arguments for and against the pastor's wife serving as Sunday School superintendent?

2. If the pastor decides to teach, should he be permitted to choose the class he wishes to teach or should he accept one assigned to him?

3. What can the pastor do about an *outsider* who conducts his own adult Bible class in the church but does not even attend the preaching services?

4. What can the pastor do about teachers who are faithful in Sunday School but evidence no interest in the other services of the church?

5. Under what circumstances might a pastor's active interest in the Sunday School become a hindrance to his general ministry to the church?

6
The Minister in the Vacation Church School

Great oaks from little acorns grow. What began as a Baptist city mission project in New York City at the turn of the century has developed into a world wide movement of Christian education ministering each year to millions of children. Although not as common as the Sunday School, the vacation church schools are found in rural as well as urban communities, in small as well as in large churches, in the slums as well as in the suburbs. They are growing in popularity throughout America.

The Sunday School and the vacation school

The vacation church school affords the church an opportunity to supplement the work of the Sunday School. The Sunday School provides one hour once a week for learning with an interval of six days for forgetting. The vacation school offers three hours a day for five continuous days during each of two weeks for a total of thirty hours of teaching. Some pastors are of the opinion that the children learn more and retain more from two weeks in the vacation school than from a whole year of Sunday School attendance. This may not always be so, but pedagogically there is an advantage in concentration in the learning process rather than long intervals between each learning experience. Absenteeism is higher in the Sunday School than in the vacation school. The former often becomes monotonous, the teaching falling into the same patterns Sunday after Sunday, seldom presenting anything new or especially challenging. The vacation school has a fresh and interesting approach; there is variety such as handwork, etc.

The home and the vacation school

The close of the elementary public schools at the end of the school year presents a problem to the parents. For ten months the public school teachers have shared with the parents the responsibility of supervising the children. Six hours each day a staff of trained teachers have directed the activities of these youngsters. Then comes the last day of school! The children shout for joy, the teachers draw a sigh of relief, the parents too sigh — but not sighs of relief. On Monday the emancipated school children will be their parents' responsibility. This new found freedom may become a serious problem. The public schools' safety rules regarding playing in the street and careful crossing of streets are forgotten. Dashing youth in the streets become a hazard to motorists. Released energy often eventuates in mischief. Otherwise well behaved children seem to lose self control.

Some families migrate from their city homes to lakeside summer cottages, or forest cabins as soon as school has been dismissed for the year; but many must remain at home. Through the vacation school the church offers a two-week "baby sitting service." Parents who may not be particularly concerned about their children's spiritual nurture welcome an opportunity to have a responsible institution render help through this educational bridge between school and vacation. It opens to the church a field for educational evangelism. In this instance, it is the church's objective rather than that of the parents that is vital.

The vacation of the pastor and his family

No serious minded person would question the hard working pastor's need of a vacation. The pastor whose family includes children in the public school age may perhaps feel that the ideal time to take his well earned vacation is as soon as the schools close. Some church member has perhaps offered the use of his summer cottage at the beginning of the vacation season, or perhaps the pastor has the good fortune of having a cabin of his own, or it may be that the vacation plans include an auto trip with the family to see new places or to visit old friends. What about the vacation school? Some pastors consider this vacation school as being a seasonal project not directly related to their regular ministry; so they leave the whole responsibility to others. This is both inconsistent and a selfish attitude. The vacation unit of Christian education is as much a part of the program of the church as is the Sunday School. Pastors have been known to hesitate to promote the vacation school out of fear that it may affect the time of their summer vacations. It would indeed seem strange for the pastor to be enjoying his vacation while the folks at home would be struggling with the school. Even if the pastor does not teach a class, he needs to be there for moral support and as evidence of his interest in the entire educational program of his church. He is deserving of a vacation, but he may need to revise the vacation schedule. The teaching ministry must not be neglected even for the sake of the pastor's vacation.

The pastor as promoter

The Sunday School is a self perpetuating institution. Superintendent and teachers come and go but the school continues. It establishes the tradition that pupils and teachers meet at a specific place every Sunday. Sunday School thus becomes an educational habit. Not so the vacation school. It is a seasonal project only remotely related to the Sunday School. Integrating it into the ongoing program of the church becomes difficult. Here the pastor can render real service. It may be necessary for him to take the initiative in proposing that such a school be conducted. In some churches the vacation school is the board of parish education's concern, and so it should be, while in other churches the vacation school is very much an orphan.

When plans have been perfected to conduct the school, the pastor can do much to promote it, in the church bulletin, as a public announcement and in various other ways. In some communities there is a vacation church school parade with banners and music, held usually the Saturday before the sessions start. If the school is a cooperative or community project such a parade may prove very effective. Even if the churches in a community conduct their own schools, they can still cooperate on the parade. The pastors leading such a demonstration will add prestige to the project.

The pastor as director

The Sunday School superintendent has a term of office. It may vary in length, a year or more. But being director of the vacation school can scarcely be called tenure of office. Someone is usually appointed to serve. If the church has conducted a summer session for a number of years, the same person may have become the "annual" director. If possible, someone besides the pastor should be director, but there are situations where he feels that unless he assumes leadership nothing will be accomplished. It is after all only for a brief season, although considerable time and energy must be spent in preparation and promotion. He should, however, insist upon an assistant who can take over in a case of emergency. The pastor never knows in advance when he may be summoned to some seriously sick person in the hospital or some victim of an accident.

The pastor as teacher

If the pastor is not the director, there is no good reason why he should not teach a class if requested. He will perhaps prefer to teach the older children rather than the beginners. He will need some pedagogical self discipline so that he will actually be teaching and not preaching to his class or resorting to story telling, even if they be Bible stories. The pastor will find it necessary to devote time to lesson preparation. Just because the pastor is familiar with the contents of the Bible does not mean that he is able to communicate its message to restless youth. His class may be the very ones who next fall will enroll in his confirmation class. As *teacher* the pastor should recognize the director of the school as his superior. The pastor-teacher will need to be on constant guard so that he does not consciously or unconsciously seem to assume leadership.

The pastor as chaplain

In vacation schools where the pastor's services are not needed either as director or as teacher, he should nonetheless have an active part. This could consist of something more than an occasional visit. He could serve as *chaplain,* coming daily to share in the worship service. At some service he might bring a five minute message geared to the interest and needs of the group. As chaplain he may also minister as a counselor; even children have spiritual problems. In urban schools the older boys sometimes create a discipline problem. The pastor can render a real service in such situations, not as a judge issuing sentences but as a counselor who can leisurely discuss with the culprits. Usually it is the effervescence of youth rather than lack of respect for religion that causes them to misbehave.

When new unchurched families are contacted through the vacation school, the pastor should call at the homes in order to become acquainted with the parents. If the school is of two weeks' duration, the intervening Sunday could be designated as Vacation Bible School Sunday with reserved seats for the pupils of the school and their teachers. The pastor's message should concern itself with youth and Christian education.

The last day of school

Most vacation schools present a program on the last day of the school. It is often an evening affair with the parents as guests. In many instances it is a demonstration of a day's activities in abbreviated form. The pupils' hand work and note books are put on display. This is no occasion for preaching a gospel sermon, but the pastor should be presented and share in the program with a greeting, a prayer, etc. The program should be brief, so that there will be time for a social fellowship. In some communities a general offering is taken. This should not be to defray the expenses of the school. That should have been provided for in the educational budget of the church. Since there is no tuition, parents who are not members of the church feel happier if they can in this way show their appreciation for what the church has provided for their children. The event too becomes a parent-teacher meeting when the parents get to meet the teachers of their children.

At an early date after the conclusion of the school, the staff of teachers, the board of parish education, and the pastor should meet to evaluate the results of the school educationally as well as spiritually. Constructive criticism should be recorded so that it will not be forgotten when next year's school is being planned. Pupils who have attended the summer session but are not regular members of the Sunday School should be invited to join. If, however, children who are enrolled in the Sunday Schools of other churches have attended the vacation school they should not be proselyted. Ecclesiastical sheep stealing is bad even when it concerns lambs.

Suggested readings

Blair, W. Dyer, *The New Vacation Church School,* Harper, 1939

Hall, Arlene, *Your Vacation Church School,* Warner, 1957

Ristine, Ethel, *The Vacation Church School,* Abingdon, 1947

Stafford, Helen, *The Vacation Religious Day School,* Abingdon, 1940

Stout and Thompson, *The Daily Vacation Church School,* Abingdon, 1923

Bower and Hayward, *Protestantism Faces its Educational Task Together,* Chapter IX, Nelson, 1949

Lotz, Philip Henry (editor), *Orientation in Religious Education,* Abingdon, 1950

Topics for further thought

1. Some churches conduct their vacation school at the close of the vacation season, just before the opening of the public schools. What are the arguments for and against?

2. How would you as a pastor meet the objection by Christian parents that their children are too tired of school to be enrolled in a vacation school?

3. What are the advantages and disadvantages of conducting a community rather than a local church summer school?

4. What teaching techniques may be effectively used in a vacation school that should not be attempted in Sunday School?

5. What would be the effect of charging a small enrollment fee for each child admitted to the vacation school?

7
The Minister in the Weekday Church School

The Christian owes loyalty both to his God and his government, so declares the Apostle Paul (Romans 13:1-7). Christ himself recognized the claims of government (Mark 12:13-17). If and when there is a conflict between these two loyalties, one's loyalty to God must dominate. This the Apostle Peter asserted when he faced the problem of obedience to God or to civil authorities: "We ought to obey God rather than men" (Acts 5:29). In the Old Testament we find a similar situation of conscience versus country when Daniel and his three friends, captives in a foreign country, refused at the risk of their lives to depart from their childhood faith. In our twentieth century, we have had similar situations in Norway and Germany where religious leaders were imprisoned for refusing to obey Nazi commands. Such men as Niemoeller, Berggrav, and Hallesby are modern heroes of faith.

The problem of conscience versus country becomes especially acute in the case of the pastor for he represents not merely himself, but as religious leader he represents the church. He speaks and acts not merely for himself as a Christian citizen but for the church as its pastor.

In our country with its policy, in theory at least, of the separation of church and state, we sometimes find it difficult to determine what belongs to Caesar and what belongs to God. The much discussed "wall of separation" between church and state is in no wise as total as the Russian iron curtain, but it has become a political as well as an ecclesiastical issue. Loyalty to the church at Rome or American government at Washington is at present a burning issue politically. Unless we accept as our philosophy of American life a dual personality, one part strictly secular, the other sacred, one that functions primarily on Sunday, the other on the other six days of the week, we must seek to build bridges that span this gulf between the church and state. The weekday church school constitutes such a bridge, not world famous as the London Bridge, the Brooklyn Bridge, or the Golden Gate Bridge, but a structure for thought transfer between the Christian church and the schools provided by the state. Thus it is an educational bridge.

The educator and the pastor cooperate

"The weekday church school was nurtured in the heart of a superintendent of schools who sensed the kinship of religion and education" — thus Percy Hayward refers to the Weekday movement. It is often called the "Released time movement" since the children are released from the public school schedule of classes in order to receive religious instruction sponsored by the church, this on the request of the parents.

It was the cooperative thinking of a pastor, J. M. Avann and a school superintendent, William Wirth, that brought the weekday church schools into being in the industrial city, Gary, Indiana, in 1914. There were prophetic voices earlier. In 1905 Dr. George Wenner of New York at an Inter-Church conference in Carnegie Hall proposed a similar plan, but neither state nor church were ready to act. Then, too, there had been experiments of Bible study for academic state credit on the college as well as the secondary levels in Colorado, and North Dakota; neither, however, developed into nation-wide movements as did the *released time* plan.

Unlike the Sunday School movement, the weekday church schools did not originate outside of the church under the guidance of lay leaders; the weekday school was from its very beginning a cooperative project between church and state, and between the different denominations. Originally Protestant, the idea was adopted by the Roman Catholic Church. In a number of cities the work is carried on as an *Inter-faith* movement directed in general by inter-faith committees. The Protestants teach their own children as the Roman Catholic do theirs; but in their dealing with the state the two faiths are united. The Catholic children enrolled in the public schools go to the parochial school classrooms on released time to be taught by the Catholic teachers, usually nuns. Pupils regularly enrolled in the parochial schools have fulfilled their time requirement by coming an hour early and are dismissed an hour early the day the *released time* classes are held. The parochial school class rooms and teachers are thus available for those who come from the public schools for this hour of religious instruction. Thus there is one thing upon which the Protestant pastor and the Roman Catholic priest are in full agreement — the child needs religious instruction.

Although conducted in some places as individual local church schools, the movement as such is interdenominational, and in a number of larger centers inter-faith. There are so many patterns of organization that attempting to catalog and define them might lead to confusion rather than to clarity. Every pastor interested in the weekday school should secure a copy of Dr. Shaver's book, *The Weekday Church School,* Pilgrim Press (1956).

The United States Supreme Court and the Weekday Church Schools

An act may be legal and yet not morally good. In some states gambling is legalized. A movement may be morally good and yet illegal. The Weekday movement has been charged with violation of the constitutional principle of separation of church and state. Three charges of violation have been appealed to the United States Supreme Court. The outcome of these court cases should be familiar to every pastor interested in the movement.

The first case, *The Compulsory Education Act,* was a law passed by the Oregon legislature in 1922. It was directed against parochial schools and was intended to compel parents to send their children to the state sponsored public schools. The case was appealed to the United States Supreme Court which declared the law unconstitutional. It further declared, "The child is not the mere creature of the state; those who nurture him and direct his destiny have the right, coupled with the high duty, to recognize and prepare him for additional obligations." Thus the highest court in our country decreed in 1925.

The second case, and one more generally known was the *Champaign case*. Mrs. Vashti McCollum, "an avowed atheist" in 1945 brought suit against the board of education of Champaign County, Illinois, to restrain the board from permitting a released time program. Both the Circuit Court of Champaign County and the Illinois Supreme Court upheld the weekday program, but when the case was appealed to the United States Supreme Court it reversed, by a vote of eight to one, the decision of the lower courts. Thus this Supreme Court decision of March 8, 1948, seemed to deal a fatal blow to the whole movement. A restudy of the wording of the court's opinion revealed that it was not the principle of *released time,* but rather the use of the public school system to aid in the teaching of sectarian religion that was unconstitutional. The use of public school buildings was thus banned but conducting religious classes in churches on released time was not barred.

The *Zorach versus Clauson* case was a suit brought by Tessim Zorach and others against Dr. Andrew G. Clauson, chairman of the New York City board of education, in an attempt to disqualify the weekday church school program. On April 28, 1952, the United States Supreme Court by a vote of six to three upheld the system as it operated in New York City. The winning of the Zorach case has given the movement a clear title.

The pastor as promoter

Weekday church schools are usually sponsored by a group of churches organized on a city wide basis. In large cities, like Chicago, the work is divided into districts supervised by local directors. Since the movement is church sponsored, the pastors play an important part in organization and promotion. Ministerial associations take the initiative in planning the schools within their areas. It is usually a committee appointed by the ministerial association that prepares the plans. They make the contact with the public school authorities, but only after they have a plan prepared and have been assured of the support of the churches. A council on weekday church schools may be set up with lay as well as ministerial representation from each of the cooperating churches. There are churches who prefer to sponsor their own schools. In the words of Erwin L. Shaver, for more than a decade executive secretary of Weekday Religious Education for the National Council of Churches, "In communities where there are churches strongly in favor of the individual church type of program, the wisest policy is not to attempt to pressure them to join in a common teaching program, but to respect their desires in the hope that they will join later after the co-operative pattern has demonstrated the value" (*The Weekday Church School*, page 38). Weekday cooperative responsibility has brought churches of different denominations into a functional harmony more effectively than almost any other plan. Ecumenicity must function at the local level if it is to become a reality.

The pastor as director or supervisor

Directing weekday church schools in a city system is a full-time job for one person, whether it be a clergyman or a layman. There are, however, situations where it may be possible for a pastor to divide his time between the church and the schools. In some instances it becomes an economic necessity for him to do so since the budget will not allow for a full-time director, no matter how desirable. Since very few pastors have had professional training in educational supervision, it means that they will need to do extensive reading in preparation for the task. They must be aware of the fact that it will be both time and energy consuming.

The pastor as teacher

Two of the major problems of the weekday schools are to secure qualified teachers and to select curricula adapted to both teachers and pupils. "The assertion that the curriculum is ninety per cent teacher is especially true in the case of the weekday church school" (Shaver, *The Weekday Church School*, page 61).

The teacher must be more than a Sunday School teacher, though that is a responsible position. The weekday teacher has contacts with the homes, the church, and the public school. She is a missionary as well as a teacher, for often children with no church connections, not even a flexible Sunday School enrollment, are in regular attendance in the weekday school. It is reported that a few years ago a boy after attending a few sessions in the weekday school came to the teacher with the remark, "I am glad I came to this class. I didn't know Jesus Christ was a nice man. I thought it was only a swear word." That happened in a metropolis of a *Christian* country. Dr. Shaver further states, "Foremost among the goals for the weekday church school is that of expecting its teachers to have had a training for their jobs which is equivalent to that of the public school teachers who teach the same children in the public schools" (*ibid,* p. 61) . Ideally this would mean not merely a bachelor's degree in education but a master's degree in religious education as well. They should know the *content* as well as the *method* of teaching.

Where there is a staggered program running through the five school days of the week it is possible to engage qualified full-time teachers, but where only one day a week and in many instances only one hour of that day is devoted to religious instruction, the problem of teachers becomes acute. Former public school teachers who have married and have children may be able to devote time and energy to teach one class, once a week. In other instances students from theological seminaries have been drafted into service.

The average pastor would perhaps not qualify as a weekday teacher. He knows the content of the courses taught, and he thinks that he understands children since he has some of his own; but he is a stranger to methods of teaching. Pastors who are masters in the pulpit are often flat failures in the classroom before, or in the midst of, a group of normal animated American boys and girls. Fortunately, there are a few pastors who have both talents and training along educational lines. Then there are some who have had the fortune to marry public school teachers or young women who have had specialized training in

Christian education. The greatest contribution to the weekday work by such pastors is probably to "baby sit" while their wives tend to the teaching.

But even when the pastor is qualified to teach, there are situations when it is best for him not to assume responsibility for a class. If committees, conferences, and conducting services in other parishes takes him away from his own church between Sundays, and sometimes over Sundays, it would seriously handicap the work in the class. He may demonstrate his interest in the program in other ways than teaching.

There are pastors who have made a worthy contribution both to the church and the community by their willingness to prepare themselves through extensive reading for this weekday church school ministry. (See bibliography.)

The pastor and the curriculum

Choosing a curriculum for weekday schools is even more difficult than choosing one for the Sunday School. The different theological views and denominational characteristics must be considered. There may be children from homes and churches that differ widely in their Christian concepts: Armenians and Calvinists; Baptists and Lutherans; conservatives and liberals. There is apt to be a bias if the chosen materials have been published by a certain denomination even when theological differences are not stressed. In attempting to avoid conflicts, the content often becomes so watered down as to lose its Christian spirit. It has become mere character education rather than Christian education. The pastor needs to be on the alert as to *what* is being taught. There should be a curriculum core of spiritual verities common to the belief of all evangelical denominations. In these courses we should stress the basic beliefs that unite us as Christians rather than underscoring our minor differences.

Suggested readings

Bennett, John C., *Christians and the State,* Scribner's, 1958
Blanshard, Paul, *American Freedom and Catholic Power,* Beacon Press, 1949
Cope, H. F., *The Weekday Church School,* Doran, 1921
Forsyth, N. F., *Weekday Church Schools, Their Organization and Administration,* Methodist, 1930

Gift, F. U., *Weekday Religious Education,* U.L.C., 1926

Gave, F. S., *Religious Education on Public School Time,* Harvard, 1926

Gorham, Donald R., *The Status of Protestant Weekday Church Schools in the United States,* Eastern Baptist Seminary, 1934

Hauser, C. A., *Latent Resources in Public Education,* Heidelberg, 1924

Hocking, W. E., *Man and the State,* Yale University Press, 1926

Johnson and Yost, *Separation of Church and State,* University of Minnesota, 1948

Jones, E. Stanley, *Christ's Alternative to Communism,* Abingdon-Cokesbury, 1935

Lotz, Philip Henry, *Current Weekday Religious Education,* Abingdon, 1923

McClure, Lois, *Weekday Religious Education at the High School Level,* Master's thesis, Northwestern University, 1951

Shaver, Erwin, *The Weekday Church School,* Pilgrim Press, 1956

Squires, W. A., *The Weekday Church School,* Presbyterian, 1924

Trueblood, Elton, *Declaration of Freedom,* Harper, 1955

Young, T. S., *Weekday Church School Methods,* Judson, 1924

Topics for further thought

1. Some religious leaders believe that religion could and should be taught in a non-sectarian way as a part of the regular elementary school curriculum. What do you think?

2. How do state and church cooperate in religious instruction in some European countries?

3. What do you think about Protestant Parochial Schools as a solution to the problem of integrating religion with education?

4. If you were the principal of an elementary public school where half of the pupils were released for religious instruction what would you schedule for those who remain in school?

5. What should be the content of courses taught in the weekday church schools?

8
The Minister in the Church Membership Class

There seems to be very little agreement among twentieth century Christians as to the purpose and practice of what is widely referred to as "confirmation." The Roman Catholic, Anglican, and Lutheran churches consider it a vital ecclesiastical ritual while a number of evangelical groups reject it as having no spiritual value and even warn as to the danger of substituting confirmation for conversion.

To the Roman Catholic, confirmation is one of its seven sacraments. Lutheran synods following the teachings of Martin Luther reject confirmation as a sacrament yet relate it very closely to the two sacraments they do accept, baptism and Holy communion. The rite of confirmation follows infant baptism and precedes the *first communion*. It links the two sacraments and becomes the door to *active* church membership.

Many evangelical groups who reject the idea of baptismal regeneration do sponsor classes as a *preparation for church membership*. The purpose thus becomes to evangelize, to explain the plan of salvation and to direct the individual to a personal commitment to Christ. Some groups studiously avoid the use of the term *confirmation class*. They substitute another name, such as *pastor's class* or church membership course.

Many modern parents though themselves not affiliated with any local church insist upon having their children both baptized and confirmed or "become a member of" a church. There are no family prayers, no religious instruction in the home, and in many instances not even enrollment in Sunday School. Such parents feel that the children are spiritually prepared for life and even for death if they have been provided with a baptismal certificate and a confirmation diploma.

There are young pastors who conduct confirmation classes and solemnly confirm the members on a Sunday morning in the presence of a church full of relatives and friends, but who can not give a theological reason for doing so. Since it is a tradition of the church, it must be good, but how or why, they do not know. In the theological seminary, considerable time was spent studying the two sacraments, baptism and holy communion, but a lecture or two in a class in pastoral theology on *how to conduct a confirmation class* was all the crowded schedule would permit. The student learned the *how* but not the *why*. If pastor and parents alike are uncertain as to the purpose, it can scarcely be expected that the individuals in the class shall know the purpose of what they are being subjected to, except that it is something which is required.

The theological significance

Although our approach to confirmation (or, preparation for intelligent church membership, as some consider it) is educational rather than theological, we have here a concrete illustration of the place of theology in Christian education. It is evident that if Christian education is to be *education* and not a mere *coaching,* it must deal with the *why* as well as the *how*. Turning to the New Testament, we find repeated instances of both baptism and holy communion but nothing that compares to our modern mode of confirmation. The reference to Jesus in the temple at twelve years of age is scarcely an argument for confirmation of modern youth at that age, but rather an example of youthful interest in the house of God.

In the New Testament we read of baptism, anointing, and laying on of hands. In the early church baptism and confirmation often took place the same day. In the Roman Catholic Church, the bishop or a specially empowered priest, lays his hands upon the head of the confirmed and makes a sign of the cross on the forehead with oil (chrism). This designates the bestowal of the Holy Spirit.

In Lutheran churches the rite is performed by the pastors and stresses the renewal of the baptismal vows as preparation for the first communion. Since Luther's days, it has become the practice in churches with a Lutheran tradition to baptize the infant, then prior to confirmation provide a period of instruction. The rite of confirmation introduces the confirmand to holy communion and to membership in the church.

We would advise all pastors to become familiar with the denomination's views on the purpose and practice of confirmation or introduction to church membership. You may find differences of opinion even among the pastors of your fellowship.

The psychological significance

The transfer from childhood to adulthood is not an act but a process. It is more like crossing a bridge than passing through a gate or door. There are psychological as well as physiological factors involved.

Puberty rites of various types are practiced by most primitive people. These recognize a change of status from that of dependent childhood to that of the responsibilities of adulthood. They have religious as well as social implications. We find similar rites in non-Christian religions: Buddhism, Hinduism, Zoroastrianism, to mention only a few. The Jews of today still celebrate *Bar Mitzvah* when the son becomes thirteen years of age. The term means *son of the law* or *son of duty*. It is a family as well as a religious festival.

The Protestant confirmation has a psychological as well as religious value. Although the Council of Trent recommended the age for confirmation to be seven years of age, Martin Luther suggested the age of thirteen. It was Luther's opinion that the confirmand should have mastered reading so that he would be able to read the Bible and the Catechism in preparation for the act of confirmation. Luther was an able educator as well as reformer; hence, the pattern became established in most Protestant Lutheran countries, of having confirmation at the close of the elementary school training, *volkschule*. Since very few pupils continued their studies beyond the elementary school the confirmation became a conclusion to their formal education. After this the youth went to work to earn a living.

In modern America, where practically every normal child goes on to secondary education, confirmation or admission to full and active church membership is not a terminal of the formal learning. But it still is highly significant. It is a family as well as a church event looked forward to by both parents and pupils. It is an event looked back upon throughout an entire lifetime. It is an emotionally toned occasion. Church weddings and confirmation services provide settings that touch deeply the young person's character and personality.

Confirmation Sunday is a reminder to the parents that Johnny and Jenny are no longer little children. They are not full-fledged adults, to be sure, but they are to be treated as maturing individuals. This should mean not unlimited freedom, but a freedom within parental supervision and cooperation. Parental domination results in stunted personalities, whereas lack of wise parental guidance leads to adolescent confusion and often an anti-social behavior. To the youth, the event means a new sense of responsibility and of privileges. He wants to act like an adult but the roots of his personality are still attached to his childhood experiences.

The curriculum

The traditional teaching materials have consisted of *Bible history* and *Catechism*. The former has been a paraphrase of the historical events as recorded in the Bible with a supplementary bridge between the two testaments. The catechism is a doctrinal study consisting of questions, answers, and supporting Bible passages.

Although catechisms were prepared and used in the early period of the church, the Reformation period established a pattern. Martin Luther's *Small Catechism* prepared for use with children, and his *Large Catechism* intended for pastors and adult congregations provided the general pattern for all Lutheran countries.

John Campanius, a Lutheran missionary to the American

Indians, translated Luther's small catechism into the language of the Delaware in 1648.

Among the Presbyterians, the Westminster shorter and larger catechisms contributed what Luther's catechisms did for the Lutherans. The Reformed churches had their Heidelberg Catechism drawn up by two Heidelberg professors, Ursinus and Olevianus.

In 1693 the General Assembly of the Particular Baptists in London requested a catechism to be used for the instruction of "children and servants." In the United States, the catechism of A. C. Dayton and J. A. Broadus have been widely used by the Baptists.

Within recent years a number of experiments have been conducted in preparing different materials for these classes. Not any of these have as yet been generally adopted. Some pastors prepare their own curricula and use them in mimeographed form. Some publishers provide pupils' work books to supplement the textbooks. The trend now seems to be towards a two-year course with units on church history added to the Bible history and catechism.

Each denomination zealously guards its creedal statements. It is therefore extremely difficult for any committee or board within the denomination to revise the catechism. An older clergyman accused a revision committee of trying to change the denomination's *"Christian Faith."* He was very much disturbed. All the committee was attempting to do was to restate the faith in terms understandable to twentieth century youth, but to him changing the expression would change the basic content as well. For sentimental reasons any change in the curricula must be superficial rather than radical. It is possible, however, to supplement while still retaining the traditional contents.

Methods of teaching

The traditional teaching method has been that of a drill sergeant, upholding the discipline of the class and drilling on memorized Bible passages, questions and answers. This rote memorization becomes painfully boring to both pastor and pupils, and to parents too if and when they attempt to "hear" the lesson assignment at home.

Modern methods of teaching may be used even when using the traditional lesson materials. There may be class discussion, projects, occasional written and oral quizzes. Audio-visual materials are available, especially in the area of Bible history. Make certain, however, that you are not using first and second grade illustrative materials for your seventh and eighth graders. Even audio-visual instruction should be graded and have a definite purpose. Vary your methods of teaching. It is possible to make memorization interesting. *Brief* drills and contests are helpful.

There should be a blackboard as well as good maps in the class room. At least four large maps should be provided. One map should be that of the *Ancient World,* showing Africa, Mesopotamia, as well as Palestine. A second map would be one of the *twelve tribes* and the division into *Israel* and *Judah.* The third would be of *Palestine* in *New Testament* times. The fourth map should be one covering *Paul's missionary journeys.*

Good class room discipline is not necessarily *rigid* discipline. Superimposing a military discipline upon your class may control muscles but it does not direct learning. There may be inner rebellion in spite of outer control. It is possible to permit a certain amount of humor without hilarity, to have rules of conduct without regimentation, to challenge rather than command.

Individual counseling has become a vital part of the course. These conferences should be scheduled in advance, not called at the spur of the moment when the pastor feels he should hold a session with some student because of his bad behavior. In the scheduled conference, the pastor as well as counselee should be relaxed. There should be no tension-situation. When the counselee seems willing to talk, the counselor must be willing to listen. If there are discipline problems the parents should be brought in only as a last resort. The pastor and the boy should be able to settle the problems as man to man. When it is a girl who has misbehaved in class, it may in some instances be necessary to consult the mother. Often, poor class discipline is caused by poor teaching methods.

Confirmation Sunday

Where traditional confirmation Sunday practices prevail, the fear of appearing before a public audience to be subjected to an oral examination may make confirmation Sunday a day of gloom rather than one of happy anticipation. Bright pupils may make a flashy display of their mastery while dull or self-conscious pupils may be guilty of stupid blunders. Both parents and pupils feel embarrassed. These traditional confirmation Sunday examinations are no longer as common as they once were. Oral and written examinations have been given during the course; the pastor knows what the pupils have achieved as well as where they have failed. Confirmation then becomes the graduation from the course.

The sermon on this occasion should be addressed to the members of the class. If they have attended the church service every Sunday while enrolled in the class they will not feel like strangers in the sanctuary. Some pastors request the class to sit in a reserved pew near the pulpit each Sunday. They sit together and listen together. The pastor may also require an outline of his sermon to be written out and handed to him each week. This develops the ability to listen and to concentrate during the service.

Wearing uniform robes for confirmation is a growing practice. One purpose is to reduce the rivalry, especially among the girls, and their mothers, in the matter of clothes. In some churches using a two-year confirmation program, the graduates receive the attention at the morning service when they receive their certificates. The next year's class is recognized in the evening service in receiving their Bibles which they will use during the second year. A rally of classes of previous years is often held at this evening service.

The matter of the place of the youthful church member in the life of the local church will be discussed in the next chapter. For the present we leave him with his family and friends. *This is a red letter day.*

Suggested readings

Bowman, Clarice, *Guiding Intermediates*, Abingdon-Cokesbury, 1943

Bruce, Gustav M., *Luther as Educator*, Augsburg, 1928

Latourette, Kenneth Scott, *A History of Christianity*, Harper, 1953

Maus, Cynthia, *Christ and the Fine Arts*, Harper, 1938

Painter, F. V. N., *Luther on Education*, Concordia, 1928

Plass, Ewald M., *This is Luther*, Concordia, 1948

Rogers and Vieth, *Visual Aids in the Church*, Christian Education Press, 1946.

Wattenberg, William W., *The Adolescent Years*, Harcourt, Brace, 1955

Topics for further thought

1. What has happened to the confirmands of your church of ten years ago?

2. Should the pastor receive the parent's permission before enrolling a child in his confirmation (or, church membership) class?

3. Should the pastor report to the parents at regular intervals the pupils attendance and achievement? (Report cards?)

4. Under what circumstances would a pastor be justified in dismissing a pupil from his confirmation class?

5. What values do you believe you received from your own confirmation experiences?

9

The Minister in the Youth and Adult Local Church Program

At the conclusion of the previous chapter we left the youthful church members with their families and friends. But where will they be five or ten years hence? Will they be active members in the church or will they have become strangers? Will they have any religious interests whatever? Although we cannot produce statistics for the nation as a whole, surveys reveal that churches lose a very large number of their youth during the high school years. Why?

In some circles the taking of class pictures has become a well established tradition. The pastor's study sometimes becomes a picture gallery. Let the pastor sit down in his study with one of these class pictures before him. It may be the class of five, or ten years ago. How many of that particular class does he remember by name? Which ones are active members in the local church? Which ones are members but inactive? Which ones are members of other churches? Which ones have drifted away from the church? Why?

While the three disciples, Peter, James, and John, were having a wonderful spiritual experience with Jesus on the Mount of Transfiguration, their nine fellow disciples were at the foot of the mountain struggling with a youth problem, the epileptic lad (Matthew 17:1-21). The father's complaint to Jesus must have cut like a sword into the frustrated minds of the nine, "I brought him to your disciples and they could not heal him." They had tried but they had failed. It is to the credit of the disciples that after Jesus had healed the lad they had a private conference with their Master. "Why could we not cast it out?"

They did not try to excuse themselves, nor did they resign themselves to future failure. They were anxious to know *why* they had failed. The church of today as well as the pastors should seriously ask the question, "Why are we failing to conserve our youth for Christ and the church?" There may be many factors involved. It is not merely the pastor who has failed; it is the home, the Sunday School, and the church in general.

The pastor and post-confirmation activities

The practice of admitting an entire class into the full fellowship of the local church presents both advantages and disadvantages. It insures that every member of the class is entered on the membership roll. But writing a name into the local church record is not identical with having the name inscribed in the "book of life." There may be those who have mastered the contents of the course and together with the other members of the class have recited sacred vows on confirmation Sunday yet have experienced no change of heart. Their names are on the church roster, but their lives give no evidence of Christ's control. When the final day of reckoning comes, they will be judged not by the records of the local church, but by the infallible records kept in heaven (Revelation 20:12).

Many churches show great concern for Cradle Roll babies and the children of the Sunday School, but after confirmation they leave youth pretty much to themselves. They roam the range like mavericks until in their late teens they are rounded up through gospel campaigns and are marked for the church with the gospel branding iron. Though many are reclaimed in this way, there are large numbers who have strayed from the church never to return.

Some churches have adopted a "cooling off" period between "confirmation" and church membership. The confirmands are not admitted into full membership of the church immediately upon confirmation. They are given a few weeks to make their individual decisions. In the fall, after confirmation, the pastor confers with each confirmand to ascertain his spiritual status. If he feels that he is sincere in his desire to become a member of the Christian church he invites him in behalf of the church to make individual application for membership.

In some churches that do not sponsor an organized high school age youth program, the pastors continue their contact with the members of the class by means of weekly meetings. These usually consist of a brief Bible study followed by a social hour. These studies should be of a practical rather than a theological nature. The many ethical problems of the high school group may thus be sympathetically discussed with the pastor. He does not lecture the young people nor dictate the solutions to their varied problems, but he helps them to discover for themselves what the solutions are. Whether or not the group is formally organized is not important. Upon graduation from high school the group generally becomes scattered, but the impact of these church-sponsored weekly social activities will have left lasting impressions upon their personalities. To conduct such sessions calls for much of the pastor's time and energy, but it is time well spent, for it is an investment for the future.

The pastor and professional directors of youth work

In most large churches there are professionally trained salaried directors of youth work, but the pastor must not waive responsibility. He should feel responsible for all of the activities of the church, even the youth program. He must keep in close touch with the youth activities of his church. This calls for Christian tact lest the director comes to feel that the pastor is usurping the director's authority. There are well-meaning directors who stress the recreational and social phases of the youth programs at the expense of the spiritual. Christian education of youth is not limited to Bible study, prayers, hymn singing, and testimony meetings. The social and recreational activities are also a vital part. They must not, however, take priority. And it is well to remember when planning social events under church auspices that an opening prayer and a concluding prayer does not sanctify what takes place between the prayers.

There are other directors who have a tendency to use pious platitudes and Christian clichés which in turn become a part of the youth's religious vocabulary but do not represent real personal religious experiences. This may make religion a matter of language rather than of living.

An aggressive director with a pleasing personality may unconsciously attract youth to himself to the extent that the youth program becomes a church within the church. If the pastor is middle-aged and the director scarcely more than an adolescent himself, the problem may become painfully acute. The result may be a dual leadership within the church. This situation may develop long before either the pastor or director are aware of what is happening. There have been instances where the matter has become so serious that it has become necessary for both pastor and director to resign. But a divided church is not easily united even with the change of leadership. Regular conferences between pastor and director should prevent such sad situations from arising.

The pastor educating adults

Adults Learn and Like It is the striking title of a recent book by Irene Caldwell. The title itself suggests two things, (1) that adults are *able* to learn, and (2) that they *enjoy* doing so.

The idea that adults do not learn but merely apply what they learned as children has led educators both in the secular and the religious fields to focus the learning processes largely on children. Modern educational psychologists, however, have demonstrated that although the ability to learn does not *increase* when we become adults, the ability *continues*. In fact the ability to learn may *decrease* as we grow older but it may continue until far past the so-called middle age. This discovery has promoted the adult education movement in secular education. Colleges and universities have conducted evening classes where grey haired men and women, some of them grandparents, have successfully pursued studies.

The church too is becoming aware of opportunities in adult Christian education. Aside from the training in the theological seminaries, Bible institutes, and missionary training schools, the church has in the past limited its adult educational program largely to the Sunday adult Bible classes. Earl Zeigler in his book, *Christian Education of Adults,* lists the goals of adult Christian education as formulated by seventeen denominations; although they vary in detail, there is a general agreement in terms of spiritual growth. Adult Christian education is not a mere dispensing of information; it develops attitudes and deepens insights. It creates change. But it also mediates information. Most pastors deplore the fact that even their most loyal church members are Biblically illiterate. Their Bible knowledge consists of the remnants from a fragmentary Sunday School attendance with perhaps the addition of a superficial confirmation course. The Sunday School teachers are too often *lesson* rather than *Bible* teachers. They bolster their ignorance with stereotyped lesson helps. In order to meet this crying need for further Biblical instruction, many pastors are combining Bible studies with the traditional midweek prayer meetings. The response has been gratifying. Entire books of the Bible may thus be exegetically studied.

Then there are mission study courses sponsored by different organizations of the church. The pastor is usually the one who is asked to teach such courses. Some of these adult courses may be seasonal — for instance during Advent or Lent. Some may be courses preparing for church membership or adult confirmation classes. The pastor, however, must beware lest he start more teaching projects than he can successfully complete. There are times when he must decline the invitation to launch new teaching activities. It is easy for a pastor to spread his activities out to the extent that they become superficial.

The pastor preparing for his classes

If the adult education lessons are to become more than a mere running commentary on the verses of a Bible chapter or the bare outline of a missionary biography, the pastor must spend consecrated time in his study. Not only does he need to become thoroughly familiar with the contents of the course, but he must also carefully consider the needs and interests of the individuals he is to teach.

Since most adults are not in the habit of taking notes it might prove helpful if the pastor prepared a general outline of each lecture, mimeographed it on punched paper, and provided each member of the class with a copy at the beginning of each session. The lecture sheets can be preserved in loose leaf notebooks. These outlines help to keep teacher and class thinking together as the class session proceeds.

Occasionally films, film strips, or slides may be used effectively. Make certain, however, that they contribute educationally and are not introduced merely to entertain or to fill in a poorly organized teaching program. There is a wealth of available audio-visual materials but they must be carefully selected and intelligently used. The pastor should have in his library a copy of either Edgar Dale, *Audio-Visual Methods in Teaching* or Rogers and Vieth, *Visual Aids in the Church.*

The modern adult is clock conscious. At work he punches the time clock, his appointments are in terms of minutes, the speed of his automobile is *clocked,* at least by the traffic officer. The pastor who lacks respect for the clock may soon learn that his class begins to dwindle. Adults are concerned about when the class session concludes as well as when it begins. The pastor who runs over time because he himself is inspired or he thinks the class is interested may sooner or later discover his mistake. Begin promptly and conclude promptly. Adult education sessions should in general not extend beyond one hour. Yes, *Adults Learn and Like it* when conditions are right.

Suggested readings
Bowman, Clarice, *Ways Youth Learn,* Harper, 1952
Caldwell, Irene, *Adults Learn and Like It,* Warner, 1955
Dale, Edgar, *Audio-Visual Methods in Teaching,* Dryden, 1946
Gorham, Donald, *Understanding Adults,* Judson, 1948
Harner, Nevin C., *Youth Work in the Church,* Abingdon-Cokesbury, 1942
Mayer, Herbert C., *The Church's Program for Young People,* Century, 1925; *Young People in Your Church,* Revell, 1953
Moon, Allen, *The Christian Education of Older People,* Cokesbury, 1943
Rogers and Vieth, *Visual Aids in the Church,* Christian Education Press, 1946
Wynn, John Clark, *Pastoral Ministry to Families,* Westminster, 1957
Zeigler, Earl F., *Christian Education of Adults,* Westminster, 1958

Topics for further thought

1. Why do denominations so often change the organizational patterns of their youth work?

2. Why is it usually not wise to permit the class to choose the Bible book to be studied?

3. Should the pastor be permitted to choose the director of youth work?

4. What should be the prerequisites for becoming a member of a local church?

5. What was the *Half-way Covenant* of early New England?

10

The Minister in Youth Camps and Conferences

Bernard A. Weisberger in his book, *They Gathered at the River,* traces the camp meeting movement to Gasper River in Kentucky about the year 1800. His description of these revival meetings suggests religious orgies. The sources from which he draws his information are, however, biased, some in favor of the movement, others opposed. He credits, or discredits, the Presbyterians, Methodists, and Baptists with sponsoring these services although the activities centered around certain rough hewn personalities. It was a primitive frontier expression of frenzied religious feelings.

The Methodist camp meetings common in America a century later were only remotely related to the early revivals described by Weisberger. They became the forerunners of our twentieth century youth camps. The YMCA and the Boy Scout movements have largely developed the pattern of present day Christian camps. The Salvation Army too has pioneered in providing so called "Fresh Air" camps for underprivileged children and mothers from the city slums. Christian summer camps for children, youth, and adults are distributed throughout our nation. Some of them are privately owned, others are sponsored by church groups. Large sums of money are invested in camp grounds; some are very primitive, while others are more like summer resorts. Some are called "Bible Camps" and are in reality conferences rather than camps. The program provides a maximum of services with a minimum of recreation. The English Keswick Conference is an example of the Bible conference type. The Northfield Summer conferences conducted for many years on the campus of the Northfield (Massachusetts) school is an example of a similar American conference. Outstanding clergymen from England, Scotland and other European countries came to this campus to deliver their sermons and lectures. American clergymen came to have their minds refilled and their souls refreshed as they listened to these servants of God proclaim the eternal truths of the gospel. This Northfield Conference was an expansion of the student conferences sponsored by the great evangelist, D. L. Moody. In this chapter we shall concern ourselves primarily with the Christian Youth Camps rather than the Bible Conference.

Christian objectives in camping

Clarice Bowman in her book, *Spiritual Values in Camping,* and Raymond R. Peters in *Let's Go Camping,* both insist that well organized camping is more than mere fresh air, good food, fun, and recreation. There are definite spiritual values. Peters presents ten goals for camping. Four of these would apply to any Christian camp whatever the age group.

1. *Wholesome recreation.* Living for a week or two in the open air surrounded by the glories of nature is in itself *recreation* for any city dweller. The camp provides directed activities, hikes, nature studies, swimming and sports of different types. It is not merely recreation; it is *wholesome* recreation.

2. *Christian fellowship.* Living together for a week as a Christian community is a spiritual as well as a social experience. The campers learn to respect the rights and ideas of others. A well conducted camp is a laboratory in group living.

3. *Christian nurture.* The devotional life is shared. There are meal time prayers, vespers, group devotions in the cabins at the close of day, Bible studies, gospel singing, etc. The atmosphere is charged with the spirit of Christ. Campers learn from one another as well as from teachers and counselors.

4. *Evangelism.* It is but natural that "evangelistic" pastors would want the entire summer camp season to be a series of revival meetings. Dramatized emotional appeals usually bring results from children and youth in terms of hands raised for

prayers, or "going forward." Juniors are especially responsive. But to what extent are such coerced camp conversions real commitments to Christ or merely a physical response to an emotionally toned appeal? After six months, what has become of these *camp converts?*

Yet, the summer camp does offer a fertile field for evangelism. Night and day for a whole week the campers live in a Christian atmosphere. Daily they are brought face to face with the challenge of Christ. The plan of salvation and the meaning of the Christian life is explained to them. The counselors give guidance in the campers' search for Christ. Without dramatic altar calls or prolonged "after meetings" the counselor and counselee are brought face to face with real values of life. They pray together; they share experiences. Yes, there are genuine conversions in summer camps, occasions when youth forms a life long partnership with Christ.

The pastor as promoter of youth camps

Since children and youth are involved in this great movement, the local pastor should be actively interested. He can do much to encourage parents to send their juniors to camp and can stimulate an interest in the high school age youth to attend. Pastors can help to sponsor camp rallies in the local church when pictures showing the activities of last year's camp are presented. Pictures are far more effective than oral descriptions. The pastor may volunteer to use his car in transporting children to the camp. When they return from camp the pastor may give them an opportunity to share some of their camping experience in a public service. This will "sell" the idea of the worthwhileness of the spiritual values of camping to older church members who have lacked confidence in this form of Christian education. Then too it gives the "new born" an opportunity to give their personal testimony of their Christ experience.

The pastor as a member of the camp board

Camps are usually administered by a board of directors. It has been deemed wise to have both pastors and laymen serve on such boards. The laymen are primarily concerned with the finances of operating the camp. This too should be of interest to the pastors, but their major responsibility is to maintain Christian standards in the program and conduct of the camp. Church sponsored activities can very quickly lose their spiritual character and become secular in nature unless they are constantly guarded. This is true especially of a church sponsored organization that operates a distance from the church that sponsors it.

If the pastor is to be a contributing member of the camp board, he must make himself familiar with camping practices and the general philosophy of camping. Much of this he may glean from good books on camping. He should devote some time each season to visit other camps to discover how they operate.

The purpose of the board is to formulate guiding principles for operating and maintaining the camp. These should not be so specific that they prevent the manager from using initiative. The principles when agreed upon should be preserved in writing. There are those who argue that between fellow Christians the word of mouth should suffice, and that written documents and contracts reflect lack of faith. Such attitudes are more pious than practical. Was not the decalogue engraved on tablets of stone? The Bible is God's words in *written* form. Written principles and contracts safeguard against misunderstanding and misquoting oral agreements, even among Christians.

The pastor as camp manager

Some camps engage managers who are salaried for the year and devote their entire time to the work of the camp. When the camping season is over, there is the storing of equipment and the repairing of buildings and equipment. Placing retired pastors in such positions may be a friendly gesture towards the pastors, but it scarcely promotes a *youth* camp. There are situations, however, where a pastor is engaged to manage the camp during the three months of the camping season. Some have proved to be good managers indeed. But they should secure a leave of absence from the pastorate during the camping season.

To manage a camp and to fill the pulpit of one's own church on Sundays is fair neither to the church nor the camp. A seminary student or a retired pastor may be secured to serve the church during the pastor's leave of absence. The function of the manager is not to police the grounds, but to operate the camp. He must be vested with authority to act, but he is also responsible for his action.

The wise manager, be he pastor or layman, will not formulate his own rules and regulations governing the camp. This is the work of a committee consisting of manager, counselors, and representatives from the campers themselves. There are certain basic rules that would apply to the entire camping season; there are others that would depend upon the age group concerned. The same rules might not apply to college age young people as to juniors. Make the "rules" suggestions rather than fixed laws. The place is not a concentration camp to be ruled by brutal force, but a Christian community directed by love. Presenting the camper at the time of registration with a mimeographed sheet of "Thou shalt nots" to be orally reviewed later in a public gathering is not conducive to a Christian camp spirit. Youth, especially those of high school age, resent being dictated to. The "don't do this" and "don't do that" creates within each individual a spirit of rebellion. Then too the "don'ts" may suggest, especially to juniors, forbidden acts that they had not themselves thought of. When youth discovers that camp rules are like rules in athletic games — not to inhibit, but to direct — they will cooperate.

Discipline may become so lax that the camp comes to resemble an anarchy more than a Christian democracy. When supervision becomes so relaxed that teenagers come sneaking into camp in the wee hours of the morning and courting couples, sometimes even counselors, sit in parked automobiles along dark country roads, or even on the camp grounds, long after midnight, one may wonder if the camp is not guilty of creating health as well as moral problems. When campers come to the morning Bible studies bleary eyed and only half awake, when they are physically so tired that they fall asleep at the evening services, one may well ask what has happened to the spiritual values in camping?

I have shared in youth camps where the conduct of both campers and counselors was such that I have felt that the camp experience was a hindrance rather than a help to the building of Christian character. They were church sponsored but the leadership was lacking. There was activity but it was not directed creative activity.

Then there are other church sponsored camps that operate with a military discipline. The manager is a "tough top sergeant," the counselors function as military police. Infractions of camp rules are handled with the objective sternness of a court martial. The spirit of the camp is that of Old Testament legalism, totally lacking in Christian love and understanding.

We have cited the two extremes, one with unlimited freedom, the other with regimentation. Fortunately the majority of the camps do not conform to either of these types, but provide wholesome, directed, well balanced youth activities. They permit liberty without license, fun without frivolity, conversion without coercion, discipline without dictatorship. Such creative camping experiences do not just happen; they are the result of careful planning and tactful administration.

The pastor as camp counselor

The success or failure of a youth camp depends more upon the choice of counselors than upon any other single factor. The young pastor is often called upon to serve as camp counselor. It affords him a wonderful opportunity of observing youth at close range. He must not think of himself as a doctor diagnosing disease and prescribing pills. His function is more like that of a guide who directs and interprets what is being experienced.

He is still a pastor while in camp. His parish is smaller, his parishioners are fewer, but he is still a shepherd. In relaxing his ministerial dignity in camp there is danger that he resorts to such freedom of action and speech that his counselees lose their respect for him. Seeing the pastor playing the part of a clown in camp may provoke boisterous laughter on the part of his counselees but it will scarcely enhance their respect for him when he appears in the pulpit of his church to preach the gospel on Sunday morning. He should share in the fun of the camp but always with a bit of a restraint. As counselor he is in need of a sense of humor as well as patience.

The pastor is counselor of a group, but the group is made up of individuals. His success as counselor will depend largely upon his ability to discern the needs and interests of each individual. Before he has spent many hours with his group, he begins to discern differences. Some are extroverts, others introverts. He may discover some potential mischief maker whose confidence and cooperation he needs to cultivate. For a pastor to spend a week as camp counselor is not a vacation. It is a strenuous task. But the alert pastor will learn much for his own benefit as well as give guidance to his counselees in developing attitudes as well as directing activities. It is a cooperative learning experience.

The pastor as camp chaplain

In many camps there is a person designated as chaplain. He is responsible for securing leaders for the different worship services. He does not attempt to do it all himself, but carefully selects those who participate. The chaplain is usually a pastor. At some camps the chaplain is chief counselor who meets daily with the other counselors to discuss problems as they arise. He should have "office hours" when counselors or counselees may confer with him. He may be the speaker at the vesper services of a junior camp. The messages should be brief, about fifteen minutes, and beamed to the interest of the audience. With a definite theme for each evening message it is possible to carry the idea into discussion sessions in the cabins at bedtime. The counselor in each tent, or cabin, directs the discussion of his group. After the discussion there are evening devotions, lights out, quiet, and after a night of rest the counselors and campers awaken refreshed and ready for a new day of interesting activities.

Whatever role the pastor is called upon to play in the camp

program, he is making a contribution to Christian education. His own life has been enriched as he has been of service to others.

Suggested readings

Bower and Hayward, *Protestantism Faces its Educational Task Together,* Nelson, 1949

Bowman, Clarice, *Spiritual Values in Camping,* Association Press, 1954

Dimock, Hedly S. (editor), *Administration of the Modern Camp,* Association Press, 1948

Drought, Alice R., *A Camping Manual,* A. S. Barnes, 1943

Johnson, Charles A., *The Frontier Camp Meeting,* Religious Harvest Time, Dallas, 1955

Peters, Raymond R., *Let's Go Camping,* Brethren, 1945

Roberts, Dorothy M., *Leadership of Teen Age Groups,* Association Press, 1950

Schindler, Carl, *The Pastor as Personal Counselor,* Muhlenberg, 1942

Sweet, William W., *The Story of Religion in America,* Harper, 1950; *Religion in Colonial Times,* Scribner's, 1942

Weisberger, Bernard A., *They Gathered at the River,* Little, Brown, 1958

Topics for further thought

1. Should our youth camps be coeducational or should boys and girls attend separate camps?

2. Under what circumstances should a camp counselor refer a counselee to another counselor?

3. Should the pastor-counselor keep up his contact with a counselee after the camp is over if the counselee belongs to another church?

4. What can a pastor do to train camp counselors for their task?

5. How should the camp program for a group of juniors differ from that of the high school age?

11

The Minister in Leadership Recruitment and Training

We are living in a leadership conscious age. We all strive to become generals, or at least captains. No one wants to be a private. Leadership has been rewarded both financially and socially. Only leaders are important. This same spirit has invaded the Christian church. We recruit potential leaders and we sponsor *Leadership* courses to train them. A few years ago a well known religious leader declared that we are today in greater need of *discipleship* than of *leadership*. He was not a cynic. He recognized the need for leaders but he also recognized that if we are to have leaders there must be those who are to be led. All Christians should be *workers,* but not all workers are leaders. Perhaps in the church we should stress less the training of *leaders* and turn our attention to training *workers.* In the ministry of Jesus, we find more emphasis on workers in the vineyard and on discipleship than we do on leadership. We need leaders in the church as well as in the state. How to discover potential leaders becomes the problem of recruitment.

That there are individual differences in temperament as well as in talents is evident to any intelligent observer. Various attempts have been made to classify differences in temperament, one of the earliest being that of Hippocrates (*circa* 400 B.C.). The terms he used have survived even though modern science has long ago discarded his theories. His four-fold classification of temperament was based upon the theory that the differences were caused by an excess of *blood, black bile, yellow bile* or *phlegm.* He used the terms sanguine, choleric, melancholic, and phlegmatic. The phlegmatic personality was a slow mover because of the excess of phlegm. We still refer to extremely calm and composed personalities as being phlegmatic. The twentieth century Swiss psychiatrist Carl Jung suggested a two-fold classification, *extroverts* and *introverts;* later a third class was added, the *ambiverts*. Although living more than two thousand years apart, using different terms to describe the differences and differing in their reasons, Hippocrates and Jung agree that human personalities differ in temperament. Not every person is a *born* leader nor can we produce leadership qualities by training where the talent is lacking. God never intended every human being to become a leader. When we try to force them into becoming leaders we are working contrary to nature. This is true in secular as well as in religious situations. More than one business executive has developed gastric ulcers and serious heart conditions because a socially ambitious wife has goaded him on to seek a position of leadership for which he had neither the temperament nor talent. He had been coached into doing what was contrary to his nature.

In the church we have tried to transform introverted Andrews into extroverted Peters, but with little success. We must recognize two facts; first, that the church is in need of leadership, and secondly, that not all good Christians are potential leaders. This presents us with the problem of how to discover the potential leaders and recruit them for training leading to service.

The local church needs leaders

The leadership of the pastor in the local church needs to be supplemented by lay leaders. There are directors of music, of children, of youth, and of Christian education in general, besides the superintendents of the various departments of the Sunday School, teachers, and counselors. Most of these are chosen from within the membership of the church. Without much concern for their native talents the church drafts its leadership and then hopes and prays for the best. Every "office" in the church is important, though some may seem more glamorous than others, and the leaders are given more public attention. The church ushers are usually not considered leaders in the church even though they "lead" worshipers to their pews. But a friendly usher may contribute more towards bringing a visitor back to the church than even the pastor's sermon or the choir's anthems. Trustees and deacons are leaders in their respective areas. Parents too are, or should be, religious leaders in their homes. In the average church we often discover unhappy situations where "square pegs" are trying to fit round holes of service. There is a real need for rethinking and refining the methods of recruiting leadership in the local church.

The denominations need leaders

Candidates for the ministry, for missionary activities, and denominational executives are all drawn from the local churches. The future pastors, missionaries, and denominational administrators are at present enrolled in some local Sunday School. The restless intermediate may be a potential church executive, the giggling girl in the junior class may become a future missionary, while the bashful boy may be a potential pastor. Discouraged Sunday School teachers might experience an emotional lift if they could peer into the future.

A recent survey of the students of a theological seminary revealed that most of the candidates for the ministry had come from small town or rural churches. Those who had come to the seminary from the large urban congregations had in many instances received their early Christian nurture in the small churches of rural areas.

The local church must not only supply its own demand for leaders but it must produce leadership for the denomination as well. This is an often forgotten phase of Christian education.

The local pastor recruits leaders

For all practical purposes the pastor is the leadership recruiting officer for the denomination as well as for the local church. The pastor of a small charge has a decided advantage in this respect over the pastor of a large congregation in that he gets to know his flock more intimately. He has opportunity to observe at close range both the abilities and limitations of the "teenagers" of his church. If he has served the church for a decade or more he has seen the small children grow into adolescents, and the adolescents blossom into adults. He has come to discover in some of his young people intellectual and spiritual resources that should be channeled into the leadership of the church. There are aggressive personalities that need to be restrained while there are talented but timid ones that need to be encouraged. The pastor tends his garden plot of potential leaders as carefully as a gardener does his rose bushes.

But what can the pastor do about recruiting potential leaders for the work of his denomination? What about candidates for the ministry and missionary work? The practice of recruiting Christian workers through dramatic appeals to college senior classes and youth conferences is usually effective in terms of numbers that respond, but such decisions are too vital to be decided on the basis of an emotional appeal. Going into "full time" Christian service is a serious matter and should not be entered into without careful and prayerful consideration. At youth conferences returned missionaries often make animated pleas for volunteers for the foreign field. I recall one instance when more "went forward" as volunteers than remained in their seats. I was both thrilled and troubled. How many realized what they were doing? How many would actually become missionaries? After ten years I tried to find the answer. To the best of my knowledge only two of the volunteers are now in missionary work. What happened? The cynic would say that the speaker's enthusiasm was transferred to his audience. There was a *group hysteria,* the individuals were emotionally stirred by hormones produced by the endocrine glands. The next day after the effect of the hormones had worn off, there was a let down feeling, an emotional hangover, the volunteers had a feeling of regret, even shame, for their unpremeditated response. We grant that endocrine glands and hormones play a part in all emotional situations, but there is more to the situation than merely the physiological response. Conscientious young Christians who volunteer under emotional coercion will suffer a guilty conscience when they realize that they have acted hastily. Publicly to volunteer for service is a serious matter. It is a pledge to God that is broken if the volunteer does not carry through. Like the man in Jesus' parable recorded in Luke 14, they failed to count the cost. They laid the foundation but could not finish.

Both the Old and the New Testaments are replete with instances when God in various ways called individuals for service. A careful study will reveal that God has no set formula or pattern for calling workers. Many modern young people interpret the divine call to be in the form of a voice from heaven, a vision, or a dream. They await something spectacular. The prophet Elijah discovered that God was not in the storm, nor in the earthquake, nor in the fire, but in the "still small voice." When God spoke to young Samuel in the temple, the lad did not recognize the divine voice. He needed the priest Eli's guidance.

The pastor of today may render a real service to the youth of his church by discussing the various ways through which the divine call may come. Examples from the Bible as well as from church history may be cited. Private conferences with concerned individuals will prove helpful. This is leadership recruitment at the grass roots. There are many seminary failures and ministerial misfits that could have been avoided had the pastor in the local church given wise counsel. It is presumptuous for a pastor to tell a young person who claims to be called of God that he is mistaken, that it is all a matter of imagination. How does a pastor know what may have transpired between the individual and his God? But when the person stubbornly insists upon the field of work to which he has been called, the pastor needs to be concerned. The sincere Christian seeks guidance from both divine and human sources.

In recruiting leadership we are too often guided by objective personality scores and intelligence than by common sense. The idea that the more intelligent the candidate is the more certain we can be of his success as a leader has led to some rather unhappy results. "Eggheads" rarely become popular leaders. They may become eminent scholars and research workers but not leaders in the popular use of the term. The most successful leaders are those with average or slightly above, intelligence, with a friendly spirit and a serious concern for the welfare of those they are to lead. The leader must be but slightly in advance of those he proposes to lead. If he forges too far ahead of them, they will lose both sight and interest in the one who was supposed to lead. We refer to Christian democratic leadership, not autocratic dictatorship whether that be in the state or the church.

The pastor directs the training of leaders

It is not enough that the church recruits leaders. She is responsible for training them as well. Whether we call the training on the local church level *leadership* training or training for Christian *workers* is not too important if we recognize the contribution made by workers who may not be classified as leaders. It might be well to sponsor elementary courses for all workers and then offer some specialized courses for those who are to become leaders. Sunday School teachers may be classified either as workers or leaders, for they are both.

So-called Teacher Training Courses have been popular in most denominations. They have been short courses of an elementary nature. Charles A. Oliver's course, very popular a few years ago, was divided into five ten-lesson units. The ten and twelve unit courses seem at present to be the most popular. Most denominations have prepared their own training curricula. Community training courses will be discussed in a later chapter. We are here concerned with courses sponsored by the local church. These training courses are administered in various ways. In some churches, young people planning to become Sunday School teachers are enrolled in a special class that meets during the Sunday School hour. Other churches provide "in service" training for their staffs by conducting two ten-week courses yearly, one in the fall, the other in the spring. The classes meet once a week for an hour. In other instances they meet once a week but in a double period thus completing the course in half the time. Some churches combine teacher training with the midweek services, devoting half an hour to worship for the entire group and then dividing into various classes for the hour that follows.

The pastor is usually the one who is called upon to teach these courses but there are instances where some well-trained lay person may be secured. Where the church has a professionally trained director of Christian education he (or she) is the most logical person to teach the methods course while the pastor teaches the courses in Bible.

But the pastor's responsibility is not limited to the training of the workers in his own church. He must also give educational guidance to those who prepare for the ministry and missionary work of the denomination. Each denomination is responsible to formulate its own training program and to establish the necessary educational institutions. Admitting ministerial candidates into the senior class of the denomination's theological seminary after they have taken their previous work in independent seminaries or those of other denominations, may be justifiable in rare instances, but it should not become a policy. Each denomination can most adequately train its own workers. Some of the larger denominations sponsor several such training institutions. The local pastor should have current catalogs of all of these schools of his denomination. He can thus be of great help to his young people who are in need of wise educational guidance.

When called upon to give a recommendation to a seminary or missionary training school regarding some candidate the pastor should be objectively frank. State the candidate's weakness as well as strength. This will prove helpful to those who are to guide him in his training. The pastor who wrote a glowing testimonial regarding a member of his church and then telephoned the next day "but I do have serious reservations" was not honest with himself, nor with the candidate and school to which he was applying. I have had occasion to read a number of ministerial recommendations and have concluded that most of them either deal with trivialities or are poetically flattering. It is possible to be frank and yet evidence Christian charity.

Candidates for the ministry are human and as such are not models of perfection. There are sharp personality corners that need to be trimmed, and there are wide empty spaces of information both religious and secular that need to be filled. That is the purpose of training for Christian service.

Suggested readings

Benson, Clarence A., *A Popular History of Christian Education,* Moody Press, 1943

Bower and Hayward, *Protestantism Faces its Educational Task Together,* Chapter VIII, Nelson, 1949

Connor, Miles, *Leadership in Religious Education,* Garland Press, 1947

Goodspeed, Edgar, *The Twelve,* Winston, 1957

Knapp, Forrest L., *Leadership Education in the Church,* Abingdon, 1933

McKibben, Frank M., *Guiding Workers in Christian Education,* Abingdon-Cokesbury, 1953

Milhouse, Paul, *Enlisting and Developing Church Leaders,* Warner, 1946

Vieth, Paul H., *The Church and Christian Education,* Chapter VI, Bethany, 1947

Topics for further thought

1. To what extent should the local church share with the pastor the responsibility of recommending candidates for the ministry?

2. Should the faculty of a theological seminary have the authority to determine whether or not a student should be admitted to the ministry?

3. At what age should young people be encouraged to enroll in local church training courses?

4. Should anyone who wishes be permitted to enroll in a Leadership Training course?

5. What is the value of granting certificates to students who complete non-academic training courses?

12

The Minister in the Educational Program
of His Denomination

"We are not divided; all one body we, One in hope and doctrine, one in charity," thus our youth sing as they are "marching on to war." But the Protestant church is not only divided; it is splintered. We have many denominational bodies. We are decidedly not one in doctrine, not even in charity. In our hymns we often express goals we have not attained. It is a hope, not a reality.

America has been the spawning pool of sects and denominations. It has been religious freedom but not always the spirit of live and let live. Early American church history records un-Christian rivalry and even Protestants persecuting one another. There were times when Protestant denominations fought one another more vigorously than they did "the world, the flesh, and the devil."

When denominational loyalty comes to mean more than loyalty to Christ it becomes idolatry. Denominational loyalty is like patriotism. It is an attitude that in itself is good but which nevertheless may lead to extremes. When nationalism coins such slogans as *"Deutchland über alles!"* or even "America first!" patriotism has become a detriment to society.

This abuse of denominationalism has caused many sincere evangelical Protestants to consider denominations evil. They find no mention of them in the Bible. Hence they must be of human rather than of divine origin. They, therefore, declare their independence of all denominations. Thus we find Community churches, Bible churches, Gospel tabernacles, and other independent groups. That they are rendering a worthy gospel ministry is evident. Within their fellowship reactionaries from denominational churches find at least a temporary refuge. Here are to be found militant ministers, supercritical "saints," holier than thou "pharisees" but also some of the most Christ-like characters found in any Christian group. These independent groups often carry on extensive missionary activities and are in most instances motivated by evangelistic zeal. They are full of life but they lack historical roots.

There are Americans who have become so "one world" minded that they have but little, if any, concern for their own country. In the words of George Canning such a one is "a steady patriot of the world alone, the friend of every country but his own." There are pastors who have a similar attitude towards the denominations of which they are members. They gladly accept the benefits of denominational affiliation but are void of any sense of responsibility towards the denominations.

The denomination in the program of the modern church

We are living in an ecumenical age, when serious efforts are put forth to unite Protestantism. Denominational mergers are either already made or are in the stage of negotiation. In spite of these mergers, the *1959 Yearbook of American Churches* lists more than 250 sects and denominations. The Baptists represent more than a score of differing groups, the Lutherans nearly as many; the Presbyterians have a dozen, the Methodists more than a score. No one would seriously contend that all of our American Protestants should be united into one ecclesiastical body. Nor on the other hand would anyone insist that we need 250 varieties. But no one is competent to advise exactly how many we do need. There are Christian leaders who would urge the smaller groups to consolidate their forces and unite officially, but who fear that if the large denominations were to unite the result would be an ecclesiastical monopoly with a bureaucracy that would stifle the life of the smaller groups. We have witnessed what the chain stores have done to the private grocery stores and the traditional corner drug store. The small country schools of nostalgic memory to many have had to give way to the consolidated schools. Mechanized consolidated farms have ruined the social life of rural communities. It is all ascribed to progress. Education and agriculture are now *big business*. Is there danger that church consolidation may lead to regimented religion with freedom of worship reduced to a minimum? We are merely asking.

Denominations differ as to their types of administration. Some are democratic to the extent that the autonomy of the local church, no matter how small, is respected. Others have a centralized control that reaches out to direct the local churches and their pastors. There are bishops and superintendents. The denomination, no matter how administered, is a fellowship of churches even as the local church is a fellowship of believers. A group of churches can successfully undertake projects cooperatively that individual congregations dare not even attempt. In unity there is strength.

The pastor should serve his denomination as well as his church. Success in his parish should not cause him to become so self-centered and local in his ministry that he neglects his responsibility to his denomination.

The denomination provides educational programs

Most denominations provide patterns for an educational program from the cradle roll through the graduate theological seminary. Besides the local parish education this includes colleges, missionary training schools, training courses for nurses, and theological seminaries, which are now largely graduate schools. These educational projects are directed by administrators called and salaried by the denomination, but the policies are formulated by elected boards supplemented by commissions and committees. These administrators are frequently former pastors. The dean of the seminary and president of the college is usually a clergyman. The faculty members of the seminary are in most instances former ministers or missionaries. The denomination's president is a clergyman and most of the executives who work with him are ministers of the gospel.

The membership of the elected boards consists largely of pastors. That the ministerial boards should be thus constituted is natural, but there has been criticism that the boards of the denomination are dominated by the clergy. The current movement to promote lay leadership should insure a proper balance of clergy and laity in the boards of the future.

These boards in some instances meet monthly while others meet quarterly. These sessions sometimes continue for several days making it difficult for a layman to attend because of his secular work, while a pastor can more easily get away from his parish for a few days between Sundays. Serving on these boards brings the pastor into closer touch with the program of his denomination. A few hours, or a few days fellowship with other pastors serving on the board is in itself a refreshing experience. When the pastor returns to his parish after many long hours in the sessions he will be physically tired but mentally refreshed. As a board member he has not merely contributed ideas but his own mind has been stimulated. He has come to recognize that the work in his parish is an important part of the work of his denomination. Mental cross fertilization is an essential by-product of board meetings. The pooling of parish experiences in Christian education often results in composite patterns that prove to be practical. In order to be effective, denominational programs of Christian education must be tried and tested in the parish.

Problems in administering the denominational program

One of the difficulties is sectionalism. The churches west of the Rocky Mountains do not always see eye to eye on educational matters with the churches in New England, while the churches from the Prairie states may differ from both. In some denominations the great difference is between the *North* and the *South*. The scars of the Civil war fought a century ago refuse to heal, largely because they are continuously being irritated.

Then there are theological differences especially within the clergy. Even denominations with formal creeds will have differences of interpretation. Pastors gravitate to theological cliques. In boards that plan the Sunday School curricula this may become a serious problem. What view of this or that doctrine shall be incorporated into the Sunday School lessons? The result may be studiously avoiding debatable doctrines or else compromising until the doctrine loses all meaning to the teachers as well as to the pupils.

There is the competition with the publishing houses of other denominations or independent publishers. Preparing and publishing church school lesson materials whether it be for the Sunday School or the vacation school is an expensive venture. Poor print jobs on cheap paper is scarcely worthy of *Christian* education. On the other hand, producing ideal materials means either a financial subsidy or pricing the materials out of the range of the consumers. Bound readers for the older children are desirable, but they are expensive. Colored picture lessons for the smaller children likewise are costly. Churches are willing to sacrifice in order to send the gospel to foreign fields but they become terribly thrifty when asked to invest some extra dollars in improved materials for propagating the gospel in the home church. It is as though they were auctioning off the Christian education of their own children and youth to the lowest bidder. Parents, even Christian parents, who buy expensive clothes for their children, who do not hesitate to purchase some desired toy, and who are generous in giving their children spending money, complain when asked to spend a dollar or two for attractive materials for Christian education.

Since the cost of printed materials depends largely upon the size of editions, the small denominations are at a disadvantage. There are three avenues of action open to them; first, secure a denominational subsidy; second, cooperate with some other small denomination in a publishing venture; or third, make use of materials published by other denominations or independent publishers. With the attractive, colorful books available in the secular field, the church cannot afford to resort to second or third rate materials for Christian education. We should secure the best even at a sacrifice.

Although the competition in publishing and selling materials for Christian education is acute, there is an even greater problem. The large denominations and independent publishers can afford to engage full time professionally trained curriculum builders while the smaller denominations must assign this important creative work to amateurs, pastors, pastors' wives or perhaps school teachers. Occasionally there are professionally trained lesson writers in the smaller denominations, but not often. These willing workers learn by doing but often the results of their efforts are far from ideal.

Pastors who are elected to serve on denominational boards are chosen not because of aptitude but because they had friends on the nominating committee. They have had no previous training for the work which is the responsibility of the board to which they have been elected. Half of their period of service has expired before they appreciate what it is all about. When they have advanced enough in understanding to be able to contribute, their term as board member has expired and they retire in order that other novices may take their places. This is a process of education as far as the members are concerned, but it is a retarding factor in the progress of the educational program assigned to the board.

Since membership on the educational boards is largely a matter of popular votes rather than of qualifying tests, each elected member should be given a printed, or at least mimeographed, directive stating the nature and scope of the work of the board and an outline of the responsibilities of each member. He would then come to the first session of his board with some familiarity with its functions. Whether the pastor becomes a member of some board or not he is nevertheless responsible for the educational ministry of the denomination. As a delegate he casts his ballot for candidates. As a pastor he can influence his congregation in their attitude towards the educational program of the denomination. The local pastor is a key person in the work of the denomination.

The pastor represents his denomination in the local church

Whether or not the pastor is elected to a denominational board, he is nevertheless the denomination's representative in his own church. He should have in his study a complete set of educational materials provided by the denomination. It would be a good financial investment to provide each pastor with a "sample kit" of available materials. Often the local pastors are more familiar with lesson materials produced and distributed by independent publishers than they are of the offerings of their own denomination.

Some pastors attempt to coerce the leaders of the church into adopting the materials published by their own denomination, but "a man convinced against his will, is of the same mind still." When the teachers use a certain "brand" of lesson material because it has been forced upon them, they are apt to use them poorly. There are times when the pastor should suggest that the board of Christian education invite some person from the denominational headquarters to demonstrate the use of the materials, especially if it is a new or a revised series.

For the pastor to claim perfection for the educational program and products of his denomination would be folly. Curricula, no matter how acceptable, need periodic revision. A frozen curriculum eventually becomes a fossil. Local church leaders do not want their denominations to think *for* them but rather to think *with* them. When weaknesses are discovered in the curriculum the pastor should feel that it is his duty to convey that information to the curriculum makers of his denomination. It is the local church that is the testing ground for the materials. What may be ideal in a large urban Sunday School may not be adaptable at all to a small rural school.

The pastor is the link between the local church and his denomination's headquarters. In order to fulfill this mission he must be informed on both levels; the local church's needs and interests, and the denomination's program and provisions.

Suggested readings

Betts, George Herbert, *The Curriculum of Religious Education*, Abingdon, 1924

Betts and Hawthorne, *Method in Teaching Religion*, Abingdon, 1925

Chisler, John Q., *Christian Teaching in the Churches*, Abingdon, 1954

Landis, Benson Y., *1959 Yearbook of American Churches*, National Council, 1958

Lankard, Frank, *A History of the American Sunday School Curriculum,* Abingdon, 1927

Miller, Randolph Crump, *Education for Christian Living,* Prentice Hall, 1956

Newbigin, Lesslie, *The Household of God,* Friendship Press, 1953

Vieth, Paul H., *The Church and Christian Education,* Bethany, 1947

Zenos, Andrew C., *Compendium of Church History,* Presbyterian, 1938

Topics for further thought

1. What is the difference between a *sect* and a *denomination?*

2. When is a denomination too small to function effectively?

3. What are the main disadvantages of having denominational boards made up largely of pastors?

4. How could candidates for boards be "screened" before having their names on the ballot?

5. Under what circumstances might a pastor be guilty of neglecting his church for the sake of the denomination?

13

The Minister in Interdenominational Christian Education

In the previous chapter we stressed denominational loyalty. But this loyalty may be carried too far. Pastors as well as local churches may become ecclesiastical isolationists. In the world at large we are wrestling with the problem of coexistence, how to preserve our national identities and yet live in peace with one another. The "cold war" age is not an era of peace and good will. After the first world war we observed November 11 as *Armistice* Day; it did not celebrate peace but rather the cessation of war, as the word *armistice* suggests. During the score of years between the first and second world wars, we continued to observe Armistice Day but national hatred and jealousies were smoldering until they broke out into open flame in the second European holocaust. With billions of dollars spent for munitions in "peace" time we can scarcely look forward to world peace and international brotherhood in the immediate future.

The un-Christian rivalry between local churches and denominations in the world today does not reflect the spirit of Christ who prayed for his disciples "that they all may be one." The disciples had different personalities but the Master was concerned that they preserve *unity in diversity*. As Protestants we worship the same God, believe in the same Christ, are directed by the same Holy Spirit, read the same Bible, and have the same heaven as our ultimate goal. If we are to live together in heaven throughout eternity, we should learn to live together on earth now.

The pastor who when preaching on the text of the Father's house with many "mansions" interpreted them as being denominational quarters, one for the Baptists, another for the Methodists, and still another for the Lutherans, etc., was carrying his denominationalism into the great beyond. A retired missionary in giving a meditation based on the same Bible passage referring to Phillips version remarked "I don't like Phillips expression 'many rooms.' I don't want a heaven that resembles a huge hotel where I will be assigned to my room. I want heaven to be a place of fellowship." Missionaries are often more interdenominational in spirit than are local pastors. They are world conscious rather than parish conscious. On the foreign field we find more denominational cooperation than we do in the so-called "Christian" home land.

*Interdenominational cooperation must
function on the local level*

Denominational cooperation may be discussed at national conventions. Flowery resolutions may be unanimously adopted, but it is at the level of the local church that such cooperation operates. If we continue to build denominational fences in the local areas, removing them at the national level will be but a meaningless gesture. Union services conducted on Thanksgiving Day and during Holy week are cooperative efforts, but the results are not always what was intended. When on Thanksgiving Day the performance of the choir is critically compared with "our choir" last year, or on Good Friday the neighborhood pastors share in brief messages during the three hour service while the audience acting as self appointed judges decide which church has the most eloquent preacher, the spirit of unity becomes very superficial.

Union evangelistic campaigns both city wide and sectional have proved helpful spiritually to all cooperating churches. It is a testimony to the world at large of Christian unity. But when local churches become so statistically minded that their main concern is the number of new members added to their respective churches as compared to the gains made by other participating churches, we sense an un-Christian selfishness.

In chapter seven, we indicated the possibilities the weekday church school program offers by way of ecumenical cooperation. Leadership training is another field where denominational cooperation is both possible and practical. A community *leadership* school has an appeal especially to young people. A small church conducting its own school could offer but one course whereas in a community school there could be several courses offered, making possible a choice.

National associations of Christian education

Interdenominational associations of Christian education usually sponsor leadership training. The patterns are usually the same, short units that become cumulative towards certificates. These certificates have no academic value but they are nevertheless cherished tokens of achievement.

The oldest Sunday School association in America dates back to 1824 when through a merger of several other organizations The *American Sunday School Union* was founded. In 1839 the union published a guide to its teachers, *The Teacher Taught,* which was teacher *guidance* even if not what we today would call *training*.

The lay leaders in the American Sunday School Movement during the early part of the twentieth century were men like H. J. Heinz, Marion Lawrence, John Wanamaker, and Russell Colgate. They were not professionally trained in Christian education but they were great promoters of the Sunday School. When in 1922 the *International Council of Religious Education* was organized its leadership became largely professional workers. This raised the academic standards of the training courses. The council has contributed much in the way of leadership education. A *Leadership Education Curriculum Handbook* is available listing more than a hundred courses. Recommended textbooks are listed as well as leaders' guides. When taught by certified instructors, *certificates of progress* are issued to students successfully completing the course. These are short term courses, the *first series* covering five hours of class time, the second series ten hours. The courses cover teaching content as well as methods. Each cooperating denomination is encouraged to add to these standard courses other units that deal with the denomination's history, policy, and beliefs. These standard courses may be offered in four ways: (1) home study, (2) leadership classes, (3) institutes or conventions, and (4) worker's conferences.

The Southern Baptists have developed an effective leadership program for their own churches. It stresses evangelism in addition to teaching methods. Churches of other denominations have found these courses helpful. The colleges of the Southern Baptist Convention have contributed much in the promotion of leadership training. The convention now includes seven million members in their Sunday Schools.

A strong feeling among evangelical churches that the leadership of the International Council was in the hands of the liberal wing of the church resulted in the formation of the *Evangelical Teacher Training Association* in 1931. Clarence H. Benson, a member of the faculty of the Moody Bible Institute, became the chief executive. The curriculum consisted of Bible courses taught at the Moody Institute plus additional courses in methods and administration. Dr. Benson published a book entitled *"An Introduction to Child Study."* This together with two other of his books, *The Sunday School in Action* and *A Popular History of Christian Education,* became the basic textbooks for the program. Certificates are granted when the courses are given by approved teachers.

Community cooperative church organizations

Most cities have at least one ministerial association. In some instances there may be two, one representing the conservative churches the others the more liberal group. In the large cities there may be a city wide church federation with local ministerial associations in the different areas. Some pastors hold a dual fellowship, one in the conservative group for theological reasons and one in the more liberal assembly for practical reasons. Since Monday is traditionally the pastor's weekly holiday, these ministerial meetings are usually held on Monday morning. After the strain of Sunday, the ministers can relax, tell stories, discuss politics, and share Sunday experiences. Matters of moral and ethical nature that concern the spiritual welfare of the community are discussed, and often united action is taken. In some instances, the ministers have reserved the gymnasium at the local YMCA where they can play volley ball, basket ball, or engage in some other physical exercise. These servants of God learn to play together as well as pray together. They return to their respective churches not any less loyal to their own parish but with a feeling of comradeship with the pastors of the neighboring churches. Such experiences create a spirit of denominational cooperation rather than competition. If they are to reach the youth of the community with the gospel of Jesus Christ, they must share the responsibility.

County and city wide interdenominational Sunday School associations have become a tradition. The Sunday School conferences of early decades of our century are being revived. Many of them are rallies rather than educational conferences, but they generate enthusiasm for the teaching ministry. There are a number of laymen who feel that many of the so-called Sunday School conferences have become so professional in spirit and language that they have lost most of their inspiration. The recently organized *National Sunday School Association* is an attempt to regain this evangelistic fervor and still retain a respectable professional attitude. Organized in 1946, it is yet in its infancy. Although not officially affiliated with the National Association of Evangelicals, it does receive promotional support. Although organized on a national basis, its administration is divided into areas.

Advantages in interdenominational cooperation

There is inspiration in numbers. When workers from a small church come to a conference or convention where there are hundreds of workers from other churches, both large and small, they come to sense a feeling of fellowship. They are a small part of a great work, but they really have a share in the total work. They return to their respective churches with new ideas and new inspiration.

Interdenominational leadership training projects mean that with a large enrollment a number of courses can be offered. The students may choose a course with special appeal. There is a possibility of engaging experts to teach some of these courses, the expenses of securing them being shared by all concerned.

Then there is the exchange of ideas between fellow students. They share experiences and experiments. The courses become enriching experiences. The timid teacher develops self-confidence, she feels more sure of herself. The "cocky" teacher feels less secure. He learns that his way of doing things is not the only way. The courses result in a leveling process.

Disadvantages in interdenominational cooperation

There is sometimes a tendency for the larger churches, especially if they represent large denominations, to want to dominate. This creates, in the representatives from the smaller churches, a feeling of inferiority. It may merely be the imagination of the sensitive souls from the small churches, but even imagination may lead to inferiority complexes.

Then there is the attraction of the well-equipped church with a host of young people as compared with the church with a bare minimum of equipment and a handful of young people. There will generate a subtle sense of envy, and a desire to transfer one's affiliation to the larger group. The larger church has no intention of sheep stealing. The sheep merely think the grass is greener on the other side of the fence. So the lambs slip through the half open gate.

The expert who comes from outside the group is very apt to think in terms of ideal situations where large churches have adequate facilities and equipment. Very little of what is discussed would apply to the small church. The results would be confusing rather than helpful.

There is still one other problem, that of teaching content courses (Bible) to representatives from churches with differing theological backgrounds. There may be Armenianism versus Calvinism. There may be differences in soteriology, eschatology, and the meaning and use of the sacraments. There may be different interpretations as to the inspiration of the Scriptures. There may be in the same class members from ultra conservative and from extremely liberal churches. What shall the teacher of such a theologically heterogeneous class do? Shall he try to present the different views and permit the members of his class to decide for themselves? Shall he present his own views? If he attempts to avoid everything controversial, the teaching will be so diluted that it will have but little value.

The pastor's place in this program of cooperation

In many of these cooperative training schools there is a dean who directs the program. He is usually a pastor. In some communities the pastors take turns at serving as deans. In some schools the pastors conduct the content courses. One solution to the problem of differing theologies is to have the methods courses taught cooperatively but the content courses taught by the pastors in their respective churches. If they are not teachers, the pastors should show their interest by enrolling in some of the methods courses. It will give them a better understanding of the educational ministry in their own churches.

In his dealings with denominations that differ widely both as to theology and church administration, the pastor need not compromise. It is quite possible to cooperate without compromising on major matters. The militant pastor is often the greatest hindrance to denominational cooperation. The Apostle Paul would certainly not condone compromise on basic doctrinal matters, yet he advised the young pastor Timothy that "the servant of the Lord must not strive; but be gentle unto all men, apt to teach, patient; in meekness instructing those that oppose them" (II Timothy 2:24).

Suggested readings

Bower and Hayward, *Protestantism Faces its Educational Task Together,* Chapter VIII, Nelson, 1949

Gwynn, Price H., *Leadership Education in the Local Church,* Westminster, 1952

Lippitt, Ronald, *Training in Community Relations,* Harper, 1949

Lotz, Philip Henry (editor), *Orientation in Religious Education,* Chapter XXXI, Abingdon, 1950

Miller, Randolph Crump, *Education for Christian Living,* Chapter VIII, Prentice Hall, 1956

Murch, James DeForest, *Christian Education in the Local Church,* Standard Publishing, 1958

Swearingen, Tilford T., *The Community and Christian Education,* Bethany, 1950

Vieth, Paul H., *The Church and Christian Education,* Chapters VI, VII, Bethany, 1946

Topics for further thought

1. What are the advantages of securing leadership course teachers from other communities?

2. What doctrines would probably prove to be the most debatable in an interdenominational class in your community?

3. Could courses in methods of teaching prove equally helpful to teachers no matter how conservative or how liberal they are doctrinally?

4. Should academic standards be as high in church schools as in public schools?

5. Why do older teachers often object to new methods?

14

The Minister in the Educational Plant of the Local Church

Mark Hopkins at one end of a log and a boy at the other is often cited as an ideal learning situation. It pays tribute to both the teacher and the pupil, but the log too plays a part. Were it not for the log the two would not be in a teacher-pupil situation. In this chapter we shall concern ourselves primarily with the log, the school building. In the Christian church our educational plants are largely patterned after those of public education.

The much maligned one room *red* country school house, that was usually white, is rapidly disappearing. The many room consolidated school is taking its place. Those of us who received our rudiments of learning in the little country school house may have missed many modern educational fads and frills, but we became grounded in the fundamentals. The old fashioned country school teacher has been subjected to much sophisticated ridicule but she contributed much to the culture and character of modern America. She did not have a degree in education, she did not belong to a teachers' union, her salary was pitifully small, but she served her nation and community faithfully. We are not recommending that we return to primitive educational patterns, but we do feel that modern educators should humbly pay their respects to that passing American tradition, the one room country school and its teachers.

John Dewey, the American educator, was not long ago heralded as the great prophet of American education, its emancipator. His dictum that "education is a process of living and not a preparation for future living" became the cornerstone for progressive child centered education. As a result, the social sciences began to crowd the natural sciences with their exacting laboratory techniques. Robert Ulich of Harvard in his book *Fundamentals of Democratic Education* in comparing the social sciences with the study of languages concludes, "Many children leave the course in current events more confused than they entered, while the language courses at least help to develop thoroughness and exactness."

Since the launching of the Russian Sputnik, America has come to evaluate critically its educational philosophy. Now John Dewey has become the educational villain who weaned us away from the natural sciences and lured us into progressive social centered patterns of education. Now the cry is, "We must train scientists in order to compete with the Russians."

Within recent years there has developed a mania for elaborate public school buildings. Communities have vied with one another in their school building programs. Many of the taxpayers' dollars are invested in elaborate buildings. Much political propaganda is wrapped up in the pleas to the federal government as well as to the individual states not for funds for *education* but for *buildings*. That there is need for adequate educational facilities is evident, but one need not be a thrifty Scotchman to discern that the sky rocketing cost of school buildings is not altogether due to increased cost in materials and men but in luxurious extras that contribute nothing to the quality of the education provided for the children of the taxpayer. Coming back to Mark Hopkins and the log, the educational log is necessary but need it be of mahogany or black walnut?

During the reformation era the education sponsored by the church was formulated by such leaders as Calvin and Luther. Within the past century the influence of secular educational philosophers has tended to establish patterns in the field of Christian education. The influence of John Dewey, William Kilpatrick, and Harold Rugg was reflected in the social centered curriculum of the more liberal wing of the church. For a time the Bible was by-passed and the lesson materials used on Sunday in church differed but little from what was offered on Monday in the public elementary and high schools. The curriculum was *social* centered rather than *Christ* centered. Within the past few years the Bible has found its way back into the Sunday School curriculum even in theologically liberal groups.

We are again being influenced by secular education in the elaborate building program. Educational annexes to church buildings and separate Christian education structures are springing up throughout our nation like mushrooms. Conservative and liberal churches alike have become Christian education building conscious. Whether the new church is located in the urban or the rural area, whether it be Gothic, Romanesque, or Modern Functional in architectural style, it includes class rooms. The church of today recognizes the place of Christian education in its program. We are in danger, however, of mistaking good facilities for good education. Some years ago I was visiting a small church with very limited educational facilities. The pastor invited me to visit a neighboring large church with all of the most modern educational equipment. I was quite impressed, as he knew I would be. I sensed that he felt a bit apologetic about his own little church. After we had completed our tour of this modern church and were about to return to *his* church, I turned to him and put a rather direct question: "Do you think that these teachers with all their class rooms and equipment are doing any better teaching than your staff of consecrated teachers with a minimum of facilities?" The question, I think, at first startled him. After a moment's pause his answer came in two words, "Perhaps not."

Jesus the model teacher had neither class room nor class schedule

Elmer H. Wilds in evaluating the greatest teachers of all time nominates three, Socrates, Guatama (Buddha), and Jesus. He concludes, "Jesus was undoubtedly the greatest of the three." We know he was unique. From our twentieth century educational standards Jesus was poorly equipped to teach. He held no professional degree, he had no class room, nor did he have a fixed class schedule. He did not even have a curriculum. Yet those who heard him teach were astonished at his teaching "for he taught them as one who had authority, and not as their scribes." It was his character rather than his curriculum that impressed his disciples. He not only *taught* truth; in his own words he *was* the truth. He did not teach Hebrew history at one hour, the teaching of the prophets at another hour and ethics at still another. His curriculum was integrated. His teaching schedule included twenty-four hours of the day. At midnight he taught Nicodemus, at noonday the Samaritan woman. He needed no particular class room for he taught wherever he might be, at the seaside, on the mountain, at a publican's dinner, or in the home of Mary and Martha.

The early universities had neither campus nor classrooms

The early European universities were quite different from our twentieth century American colleges and universities. They had no campus with imposing class rooms, libraries, gymnasiums, dormitories, chapels, and athletic fields. They consisted of a band of scholars who together with their teacher sought learning. If a "college city" did not grant what the scholars wanted, they moved to another city. There were no educational endowments. The students often had to resort to begging bread in order to live.

Our modern American colleges and universities have large campuses with modern class rooms, dormitories, dining halls, athletic fields, gymnasiums, etc. Many of them are heavily endowed. Some of them resemble country clubs rather than educational institutions. Thus the pendulum has swung.

The twentieth century American church builds for education

The early European churches were not planned with education in mind. They represented religious symbolism in their architecture. The great cathedrals were demonstrations of religious art. The pietistic movement introduced the chapel and the meeting house but their purpose was informal worship rather than formal Christian education.

The Sunday School movement of the late eighteenth century

created a keen interest in work with the children. In England the movement was largely outside of the organized church. Even in America where the Sunday School was adopted by the church, it became a matter of fitting in classes wherever possible into the structure of the church. It was not before the 1860s that the churches were built with education definitely in mind. The first of these innovations was the *Akron* type of church building. It was designed by Lewis Miller, the inventer of the Buckeye Mower and Reaper. Associated with him in the planning was John H. Vincent, a Methodist clergyman. For a few years while the Uniform Lessons were popular this Akron (Ohio) type of church flourished. The assembly with its lively music and stirring talks by the superintendent or pastor, or perhaps a visitor, provided an evangelistic approach to the entire school. The class stalls or "cubby holes," where the teachers were closeted with their pupils during the lesson session, in many instances became more like prison cells than class rooms. With the advance of graded lessons and departmental worship, the plan no longer proved practical. A few Akron churches remain but more as church architecture curiosities.

It was after the first world war that the American churches began to evidence a real interest in making provision for the Christian education of the local church. The addition of Sunday School annexes to the church buildings often resulted in architectural monstrosities. In some instances separate education buildings were erected. When new churches were built provision was made for class rooms. This was true of both conservative and of liberal churches. In meeting these growing demands for class rooms, chapels, etc., many mistakes have been made. Inexperienced but sincere Christian workers have drawn up plans without consulting experienced architects. The results have often been glaring errors in planning and construction. It is often wise to dispose of an old church building and to build a new structure with the desired facilities included rather than to try to save money by adding new units to the old. Too many compromises have to be made, and when the remodled plant is complete it is far from ideal.

The pastor's place in planning the educational plant

More than one pastor has met his Waterloo in pushing a church building or remodeling project for which neither he nor the congregation was prepared. A pastor about to enter upon such a project would do well to remember the Latin proverb *festina lente* (make haste slowly). He must serve both as a stimulant and as a tranquilizer. There are church members who are always satisfied with the status quo. They prefer what they are accustomed to. Then there are others who are neurotic agitators for change. In dealing with these extremes the pastor needs tact, wisdom, and patience. If he were to wait until every member of his congregation was enthusiastic about building, he would perhaps never attain a unanimous approval. There are some individuals who are lukewarm, if not altogether opposed to any project that involves the spending of money but when a project is under way will give a hearty support.

The pastor may refer to "my church" when he talks to other pastors but he must remember that it is not he but the congregation that is sponsoring the undertaking. It is "our church." The detailed task of planning must be the responsibility of a building committee but the congregation should be informed of the progress in planning from time to time. The building committee is not a secret society but a small group acting for the church and thus responsible to the congregation as such.

The matter of cost must be dealt with intelligently. The pious phrase, *launching out on faith,* may sometimes prove to be *irresponsible folly.* When a congregation assumes such a crippling debt through a building enterprise that it can scarcely raise money to pay the interest, much less reduce the debt, one begins to wonder if it was *faith* or *folly.* On the other hand a reasonable debt may prove to be a real investment for the future.

The pastor in all probability did not study architecture in college but he can acquire valuable information through the study of books on church architecture. It is a wise investment to engage a good architect. Make certain, however, that he is interested in the functional phase of the structure and not primarily concerned with a beautiful sanctuary. There are sad examples throughout our land of large sums of the Lord's money that have been invested in sanctuaries with art glass windows and a confusing array of symbolism meaningless to the worshipers and sometimes even to the pastor. This beautiful sanctuary is used for worship one hour once a week. When a visitor asks about the absence of class rooms and teaching facilities he is informed that they hope to have them later. But how much later, five years, ten years, or even twenty?

The pastor should be an ex officio member of the building committee but he should not play the part of a dictator. He may subtly suggest and at times wisely warn. For the sake of peace it may be necessary for him to resign himself to a compromise on minor matters. The pastor and the committee will want to visit new churches as well as study blue prints. Visiting a church building on Saturday afternoon may be convenient for the committee but before any decision is made a visit should be made Sunday morning when the Sunday Church School is in action. "Bottle necks" in corridors and at exits may be discovered that would never have been suspected on the Saturday visit. Pastors, directors, superintendents, and teachers may have valuable comments on mistakes in planning as they now see it. "If we were to do this again," is often an introduction to criticism of some sort. Rarely will you find an educational plant so perfect that there are not some weaknesses. Make an appointment with the pastor and the director of Christian education, or the Sunday School superintendent at some time when they can give you something more concrete than a few hasty comments.

Most pastors are interested in a beautiful sanctuary, an auditorium, while Christian educators want light and airy class rooms, not dark cell like rooms. They want a *laboratorium*. It need not be *either,* for it can be *both.* There may be the *beauty of holiness* even in the class rooms.

A few words of warning may not be amiss. (1) Do not spend so much money on the structure that you cannot afford adequate equipment. (2) Do not imagine that a new building will solve all of your educational problems; it may create new ones. (3) Unless you improve your teaching staff, a new building will not improve the quality of instruction. (4) Saving money by buying cheap equipment may prove expensive in the long run. It is not the original cost but the upkeep that determines the real values of an investment. (5) Do not permit your new building and equipment, no matter how modern and beautiful, to become a golden calf that your staff and pupils come to worship. Even a Christian education plant may lead to idolatry. We become more impressed by the beauty of the material things than we are by the spiritual presence of God.

Trends in Christian education architecture

Although architectural styles in Christian education buildings vary greatly, there are a few general trends. The small church will in many respects differ from the large church. The rural church where acreage is available will differ from a downtown urban church where property is measured by the foot. John R. Scotford in discussing buildings for religious education (chapter 17 in *Orientation in Religious Education,* Lotz) has this to say about the Akron plan churches with their auditorium and rows of little classrooms. "About the only thing which can be done with an Akron plan Sunday School building is to tear it down and start over again." The same could be said about the gymnasiums built as church annexes after the first world war. The idea frankly was this, If we cannot hold our youth in the church with the gospel, maybe we can with athletics. The results have been disappointing. Just because young men play basketball in a structure built by the church does not mean that they are reached by the church except very superficially. Gymnasiums are hard to heat in the winter time, structurally they deteriorate rapidly. For public services the gymnasium acoustics are usually terrible. To attempt to create a spirit of worship in a place where youth is accustomed to yell and cheer at the games is futile. As a banquet hall the gymnasium is cold and drafty and the lingering aroma of athletic perspiration from previous games is scarcely an accompaniment to a tasty meal. Again quoting Scotford, "Most churches which have gyms would gladly be rid of them."

With the trend towards departmental worship there is the need in the larger churches for small worshipful chapels. The use of audio-visual aids calls for at least one room that can be made dark even on a sunny day. The use of this could be scheduled so as to give each department an opportunity to make use of it. The trend too is away from both the treacherous screens that are used to separate classes and the firmly fixed partitions. Solid walls that do not support weight and are adjustable so as to increase or decrease the size of a room make it possible to adapt the rooms to current needs. These walls shut out both sound and sight and unlike the screen do not fall down at the least provocation.

The current slogan seems to be, "Don't freeze the architectural features, but keep them flexible so as to adjust to future needs and trends." A good educational plant is not a substitute for good teaching. It is but a tool to be intelligently used.

Suggested readings

Conover, Elbert M., *The Church School and Parish House Building*, International Council, 1949; *Planning Church Building*, Interdenominational Bureau of Architects, 1945

Dorsey, Stephen P., *Early English Churches in America*, Oxford, 1952

Ferguson, George, *Signs and Symbols in Christian Art*, Oxford, 1958

Harrell, W. A., *Planning Better Church Buildings*, Broadman, 1947

Leach, William H., *Protestant Church Building*, Abingdon-Cokesbury, 1946

Lotz, Philip Henry, *Orientation in Religious Education*, Chapter XVII, Abingdon, 1950

Mason, Harold C., *Abiding Values in Christian Education*, Chapter XVII, Revell, 1955

Murch, James DeForest, *Christian Education and the Local Church*, Chapter XXXIV, Standard Publishing, Revised 1958

Scotford, John R., *The Church Beautiful*, Pilgrim Press, 1946

Topics for further thought

1. Should a church building dedicated to divine worship be sold to those who may use it as a garage, dance hall, or tavern?

2. What control does a congregation have over the use to which its former church building is put?

3. Is it ethically right for a congregation to issue building bonds that mature in twenty years when those who are now children must pay them?

4. What is the danger of the church becoming dominated in its educational plant by the patterns of secular education?

5. Under what circumstances would it be justifiable for a pastor to resign from his church in the midst of a building project?

15
Evaluating the Educational Ministry of the Church

The keyword in our American civilization seems to be progress. We are drunk with success. Books are written about successful men and women. Popular magazines feature pictures and brief biographies of those who have achieved. It is the Horatio Alger stories in modern form, poor boys who become famous. We seem to forget the financial failures of the American, Samuel Insull, and the European matchking, Kruger. At the time of Kruger's suicide, the cartoonist of one of our daily papers told the tragic story of the matchking dramatically, a burned-out match. The tragedies of military leaders like Hitler and Mussolini are all but forgotten in the dazzling glow of modern political figures. We are told that Russia's slogan is "reach and overreach America." The church too has become the victim of this success mania. Denominations vie with one another, as do also local churches within the same denominations. Our criticism, whether it be of state or of church is not that it wants to make progress but the yard sticks we use to measure the progress. Is it in terms of quality or merely of quantity? As it applies to the Christian church, is it material or spiritual growth? In the early history of the church as recorded in the book of Acts there is reported the number of "souls" that were saved (Acts 2:41, 47; 4:4). But as the story of the church continues the emphasis is on the spiritual power expressed in the life of the individual (Acts 6:8; 7:55; 13:9). Quantity came to mean less and quality more.

Can the educational ministry of the church be measured?

The pious platitude "only eternity can reveal the results of our teaching" may in reality mean "we would sooner not have our teaching ministry examined too closely." We are afraid of what we might discover. There are sincere Christians who feel that it would be sacrilege to attempt to measure objectively the progress of the gospel. They would probably quote the slogan "Do thy duty, that is best. Leave unto the Lord the rest."

The dictum "everything that exists must exist in measurable quantities" is applicable even to spiritual progress. Our problem is to find refined units of measurement that are adaptable to that which we wish to measure. We do not attempt to weigh diamonds on a coal scale nor fill liquid medical prescriptions using a gallon container.

Membership and annual budgets of the local church can be reported quite accurately. It is only a matter of bookkeeping, but that *is* quantitative measurement. Knowing the enrollment in the Sunday School a year ago and the condition of the treasury compared with the figures now reflects a gain or a loss, that is quite an elementary matter. But is not the counting of names and of dollars a materialistic measurement of a spiritual ministry? Recognizing the limitations of our available units of measurement, we shall nevertheless find them helpful. They do not measure everything, but they do measure something. When we evaluate progress, or the lack of it, we must know what we have as our goal of achievement. Unless we have definite goals which we hope to attain, we will be like a person lost in the woods spending a great deal of energy walking but going in circles coming back to the same place again. We shall establish our goals and then attempt to measure our progress fully aware that there are factors we are unable to measure, not because they are not real but because our means of measuring are inadequate. When we have measured as far as our units of measurement permit, we will with the ancients adopt the slogan *Plus Ultra* (there is more beyond).

What is the practical value of evaluating Christian education?

The business man takes an annual inventory to determine loss or profit. The student gets his report card indicating his academic progress. The government debates its annual budget whether it balances or shows the accumulation of astronomical figures in the national debt. The local church at its annual meeting presents statistics as to membership and finances but spiritual achievement is hoped for rather than tabulated. Why should we evaluate our teaching?

1. Measuring in Christian education saves us from the sin of wishful thinking. We are assured that Christian education is good for both old and young; so we carry on from week to week hoping for the best.

2. It avoids marking time. Doing the same thing Sunday after Sunday may mean no more progress than the soldier who lifts his feet to the rhythm of march music but plants each foot in the same spot from which it was lifted. The teacher may spend both time and energy, but the class makes no progress.

3. It reveals strength as well as weakness in our educational ministry. In a program of evaluation, weaknesses will be revealed but also strength. The weakness is to be strengthened and the strength preserved. A small school with a minimum of facilities and equipment may discover that because of consecrated workers it may be doing a better job than schools with far superior facilities.

4. It promotes the establishing of standards and goals. As workers we become goal conscious, the curriculum becomes a means to an end, not an end in itself. As teachers, we adopt standards for ourselves as well as for our pupils.

What are the dangers of objective evaluation?

The value of adopting high standards of teaching techniques, class room decorum and equipment is not questioned but there is one danger — that the church school becomes so academic that it loses its spiritual qualities. When the Sunday Church School becomes an almost exact duplicate in pattern and spirit of the Monday to Friday public school, we wonder if we have not lost something of spiritual value. Yes, there is a danger that in our attempt to vie with public education in establishing academic perfection we lose spiritual verities.

There is also the danger that we become overly statistics conscious. A few years ago the sponsors of an urban Sunday School launched a membership contest. They were successful even beyond their hopes. A few months after the close of the contest I met the superintendent. I asked him regarding the lasting results of the campaign. To my surprise, he said, "Never again will I be guilty of sponsoring such a campaign." The enrollment had suddenly increased, new classes had to be organized and crowded into an already well filled church sanctuary, inexperienced teachers had to be drafted into service. Quantitatively the school increased, but qualitatively the teaching ministry deteriorated. Enrollment is a goal. Even the average lay member of the church can understand figures that represent increase in membership. The same is true of financial reports. But both of these represent quantitative, not qualitative progress.

There is still another danger, that of frustrating faithful workers. Suddenly imposing detailed standards of perfection may tend to discourage rather than to encourage the members of the teaching staff. They develop a feeling of inferiority. They feel the new standards are unattainable. Faithful lay workers need to be encouraged rather than discouraged. This does not mean ruling out standards but it means that they should be practical and attainable rather than merely professional and idealistic. *What shall we measure?*

We have already suggested that changes in enrollment and financial budget can be ascertained and graphically presented to the public. There should be an annual inventory of equipment. Any new items purchased during the year should be included while a certain percentage for deterioration should be deducted. This again can be represented statistically.

But what has happened to the pupils? What changes have taken place in their character? How can we evaluate? By means of objective tests we can measure the information they have gained. But the ability to identify names, or to recall historical events, or to quote Bible passages is not the goal of Christian education. The Scribes and Pharisees could recite the Old Testament scriptures, yet they became the bitter enemies of

Christ. It is not religious information *per se* but the practical use to which this information is put that constitutes Christian education. No lesson has been mastered until it has been lived.

Pupils may solve submitted moral and ethical problems in the class room discussions, yet fail to do so outside of the class room. When a pupil cheats in an examination in Bible one discovers how far apart theory and practice may be.

The real test of the effectiveness of Christian education is not determined by the "correct" answers given in class but in the students' changed attitude and behavior. This may consist of a gradual modification of character rather than a sudden radical change. Such progress cannot be measured in such a way that the results may be recorded through academic symbols on report cards. Nevertheless they are real.

Most denominations provide standards and score cards. We would refer the reader to such books as Miller, *Education for Christian Living,* chapter 23, and Murch, *Christian Education in the Local Church,* chapter 35. The National Council of Churches through its Division of Christian Education provides a list of requirements for a church school and a score card with a point system. In Betts and Hawthorne, *Method in Teaching Religion,* there are sample score cards. A committee within the local church could devise its own score card after comparing those of other groups.

What is the pastor's place in this evaluation?

Some pastors would prefer to call in an expert objectively to evaluate the entire educational ministry of the local church. The workers of the church are usually opposed to having an outsider invade their church to tell them what is wrong. They fear that such a report would be critically negative. The thrifty leaders object to spending money on such a project since it could be a "do-it-yourself" undertaking. It is possible that self-evaluation might prove more helpful even if less professional.

The pastor and board of Christian education could and should, take the initiative in such a program of evaluation. Such a project of self-evaluation may not require the expenditure of funds but it will require the investment of time and energy of a number of people, including the pastor.

First of all there is the need of a workable measuring device. The denominational headquarters should be contacted to secure its standards and score cards. Secure similar materials from other denominations and interdenominational associations. Have a committee study them carefully. Using the denominations' materials as the basis, ideas gleaned from other score cards may be incorporated. This "yardstick" is then presented to the congregation for approval, for this is the concern of the entire church.

The actual work of evaluating should be shared by a number of workers. Each department should evaluate its own class rooms, curriculum, teaching staff, methods of teaching, etc. A special committee might concern themselves with an evaluation of the buildings used for the teaching ministry. This would include the church proper, Sunday School annexes, and education buildings.

The survey should include the vacation church school and the weekday church school besides the Sunday School. The confirmation and leadership training classes should have their share of the study. When all of the different educational units have been measured, the results should be brought together into a composite. Where are the weak areas in the entire program? The picture may prove rather discouraging, but the areas of strength should also be presented. A large chart or diagram indicating in colors the areas of weakness and strength would dramatize the results of the survey. The pastor is no doubt the logical person to interpret the findings. This presentation should be made at a public meeting of the congregation. Also, the church is often asked to contribute funds for Christian education without being given an explanation of why money is needed. The congregation has a right to know why it is called on to contribute. The teaching ministry is the responsibility of the entire church.

The board of Christian education together with the pastor should carefully prepare the program of reconstruction. It may be a three, five, or seven year plan. Goals of achievement are set up for each year. These annual goals should be attainable yet set high enough to be a challenge. They may include evangelism, in service training for workers, recruiting and training new workers, securing equipment, even a new building if necessary.

Randolph Crump Miller concludes his stimulating book, *Education for Christian Living,* with these words: "With all of our plans and standards and techniques and theological insights, it is God who does the educating. We are channels of his grace doing the planting and the watering, and the increase is a gift of God." How true! It reflects the words of Paul, "I have planted, Apollos watered, but God gave the increase" (I Cor. 3:6). We are not responsible for the growth. That is the Holy Spirit's ministry in the human heart. But it is our mission to sow, to water, and to cultivate. As God's gardeners we can not afford to be anything less than our best, using the best of tools and techniques.

Suggested readings

Betts and Hawthorne, *Method in Teaching Religion,* Abingdon, 1925

Chappell, E. B., *Evangelism in the Sunday School,* Methodist South, 1925

Heim, Ralph, *Leading a Sunday Church School,* Muhlenberg, 1950

Miller, Randolph Crump, *Education for Christian Living,* Prentice-Hall, 1956; *The Clue to Christian Education,* Scribner's, 1950

Murch, James DeForest, *Christian Education and the Local Church,* Standard Publishing, Revised 1958

Vieth, Paul H., *Improving Your Sunday School,* Westminster, 1950; *The Church School,* Christian Education Press, 1957; *Objectives in Religious Education,* Harper, 1930

Topics for further thought

1. How frequently should the educational program of the local church be evaluated?

2. What are the chief objections to Sunday School membership contests?

3. What is the danger of setting numerical goals for our program of Sunday School evangelism?

4. How may the professional growth of teachers be measured?

5. How can a teacher evaluate character growth in her pupils?

Index